MW01247533

TODAY'S WORLD RELIGIONS

by

M. Thomas Starkes

Published by Insight Press, In., P.O. Box 8369,
New Orleans, LA 70182.

Library of Congress Catalog Card Number 78-50683

ISBN 0-914520-11-3

Contents

Preface

This book is designed to aid new students in the field of world religions, not to impress renowned scholars in that area.

When I first started teaching an introductory course in world religions at a state university early in 1975, several facts soon became apparent. First, half my students were in their first year in college and had little or no academic preparation for such a course. On their first exam, they were lucky to remember to keep the "h" in Buddhism, much less remember basic differences in Mahayana and Hinayana. Second, it soon became apparent that the students were not reading the textbook. (I tried three in seven semesters.) Those who did read them found the books to be dull, out-of-date, overly concerned with history and loaded with details. Third, it dawned on me that these were *American* students, largely from a Judaeo-Christian background. They responded favorably to ideas to which they could relate. Assimilation and evaluation came much more readily when related to the students' experiences. I found that students were more interested in the "Moonies" in the apartment house next door than in any event B.C. And, to whomever it was who first said, "Living without knowledge of history is like living in an apartment or house with no windows," I reply, "Living in a house with no analysis of the present is like living in a house with no door."

With that in mind, I have tried to accomplish four goals:

1) To present a readable text with words which flow for a teenage American reader.

2) To use case studies to show that religions concern people, real people who struggle for meaning in diverse situations.

3) To include sections often omitted in other texts on world religions such as indigenous African religions, the native American scene and current America.

4) To include a simple and basic bibliography at the end of each chapter so as to offer further study helps for those who want to go one step further in the investigation of a specific religious expression.

It is my intention to revise this text next in 1982 and then again for every new student generation through this century — if God be willing.

It is to every student who ever struggled with a textbook on world religions, including this one, that this work is dedicated.

M. Thomas Starkes
January, 1978.

3

Introduction: Let's Get Going

In the United States, the most popular religion courses in colleges and universities are those offering a one-semester introduction to the world's religions. Why is that? There are as many answers as there are benefits to such a course, but basically four answers emerge from the pack.

First, the gaining of self-knowledge is a legitimate and popular reason for taking courses on world religions. As one examines his own tradition and those of others, he becomes more aware of the strengths and weaknesses of his own religious upbringing. The student makes a series of self-discoveries as he discovers who he is *not*. By seeing clearly what he is not doing and being, he can more clearly see his own identity.

Second, the new student of world religions soon discovers that others in our world behave and decide on much different premises than those presumed on American soil. Working hard, going to heaven, daily prayer, erecting buildings for religious ritual and social ministry may simply not be of interest to those facing life from a different religious perspective. Such matters as birth control, euthanasia and war may be viewed much differently by a believing Moslem, Hindu and an American "Indian." The new field of "comparative ethics" will be peopled by those students of this generation who begin to see that ethical decisions are made by separate persons for different reasons. This affords human understanding, a legitimate goal for the study of world religions.

Third, some knowledge of history helps the modern student more discerning than his shallow former condemnation of those who dress and pray differently than he. For example, bowing toward Mecca makes more sense when the events of Muhammad's life there are known. Toleration, perhaps even the granting of freedom, can result from knowing *why* other religious persons behave as they do.

Fourth, a student's first course in world religions may produce within him a sense of respect for other human beings. This respect can come only when knowledge is attained of why others behave as they do on questions of ultimate concern, those which religion addresses.

What is religion?....
The phenomenon called religion is universal. Persons worship, whether it be a Thunderbird on the top of a totem pole or one on a new

4

car showroom floor. From the Navajo reservation Indian to the Asian desert beduin religious ritual, prayer and belief are part of the human way of life. Persons are incurably religious. Humans pray, whether it be in a Catholic high mass or in an appeal to good luck. Persons develop a life-style or value system based on some prior judgments about the fundamental questions of who or what is God and other human beings. Persons also operate on some thought pattern of what the future world after death holds for him. In fact, many persons severely alter their lives on the basis of what they think the next world holds.

What is religion? How may this universal phenomenon be defined? Religion may be defined in any one of several ways. Scholars usually divide the answers into two camps, revolving around the "what" or the "why" of religious pursuits. The "what" definitions speak of religion in terms of religious behavior and the "why" in terms of the motivation behind such behavior.

Amoung the "what" definitions the student may find religion as:
1) Belief in spirit beings;
2) The worship of higher powers.

The "why" definitions include:
1) Religion is the consciousness of the higher social values,
2) Religion is a cooperative quest after a completely satisfying life.

From these definitions, it becomes apparent that religion is a complex conglomeration of the experiences of human beings in search of God and self. The definitions are as varied as the cultures and persons in the world. Yet, the quest is universasal. So, religion for persons is search of the eternal while living in the midst of the temporal. As William Newton Clarke phrases it, "Religion is the life of man in his superhuman relationships."[1]

The next question which arises automatically is, "How does one go about a systematic, thorough and objective study of religion?" Religion, after all, has been scrutinized as much or more as it has been lived.

Too often religion has been treated as the object of only one science or another. Anthropologists, sociologists, psychologists, historians and theologians have all taken their tools of inquiry to the task of disecting religious experience. What has resulted is a fragmentary understanding of religion from each of these perspectives. To understand religion, however, from only one perspective is to understand it partially at best. It is to overlook the fact that any one event or series of events is a result of a conglomerate of factors. For example, any Jehovah's witness assembly may be analyzed academically, economically, politically, culturally, sociologically and/or psychologically. To use only one such devise is to open but a bit of that event for evaluation and analysis.

To the rescue comes phenomenology, which is but a fancy way of saying two things:

---

[1]*An Outline of Christian Theology* (New York: Scribner's 1898), p.1.

1) Any religious ritual, person or happening can and must be analyzed from as many perspectives as possible to be understood as thoroughly as humanly possible. This allows every behavioral science and philosophical system to have a part in the process of understanding religions.

2) The study of religions is conducted by humans. Those humans may seek to be as objective as possible in their analysis of another's religion, but the subjective is always present. This is admitted without hesitation by the phenomenologist. Although he seeks to be as objective as possible, he knows that pure objectivity is an impossible ideal.

So, phenomenology is to be recommended as the best approach in the study of world religions because it says "up front" that this is humans studying humans, an intricate procedure at best. Fragmentation of another human being's ultimate concerns is not the business of phenomenology, for it hears regularly the gentle reminder of Confucius, who said, "He who formulates me beholds me not; he who beholds me formulates me not."

The East-West Collision....

As an example of the phenomenological method, an analysis follows of but one religious happening of the past generation, the collision between Eastern and Western religious values on American soil.

Rudyard Kipling wrote:

> Oh, East is East, and West
> is West, and never the
> twain shall meet,
> 'Til Earth and Sky stand
> presently at God's
> great Judgment seat.[2]

This may be good poetry, but stands as an inaccurate statement in light of the tremendous impact Eastern religions have had on Christian and Western thought in the past generation East collides with West every day in America. The results have been impressive. For example, the Gallup Poll on Religion in 1973 showed that 22% of the adult citizens in the United States now say they believe in reincarnation.

The question of why the Eastern religions have met with acceptance by Western people, especially American youth, is a complex one, but one which one can analyze with the broad approach of phenomenology. Among the reasons which phenomenology uncovers are:

1) *Models of nonviolence....*

During the 1940's a small man with a large mission captured the imaginations of Americans. His name was Mahatma Ghandi. Ghandi

---

[2]Rudyard Kipling, "The Ballad of East and West," *Rudyard Kipling's Verse* (Garden City: Doubleday, Doran and Co., Inc., 1945)

taught nonviolence as an effective way to change a social system marred by injustice. A young black Baptist preacher left Atlanta to study in Boston, where he was exposed to the thought of Ghandi. Martin Luther King, Jr., used nonviolence as the method of social rebellion he found effective in changing the plight of the black American. Ghandi lives on in America. He taught that truth is power. He rejected the sword as a part of social change and called for minorities to rebel one discernible, responsible step at a time.

In 1948, Ghandi was assasinated. His last words, "Hai, Rama," mean "My God!" Some say Ghandi is not dead. He has come back to life in the form of social protest as a model of nonviolence.

2) *Parallels....*

Students are discovering that there are many parallels to be found in other religions. For example, the teachings of Buddha have sections similar to the "Ten Commandments" of Judaism and Christianity. As a result, some persons have discovered that there are many truths to be found in other religious traditions. The idea that there are no spiritual truths in Islam, Buddhism and Hinduism is vanishing. In its place is the openness of search for truth whenever it is to be found.

3) *Disguises....*

An important reason for acceptance of the basic teachings of the Eastern religions in America is the disguised teaching of these groups, for example the New Thought-based *Christian* Science and the Unity School of *Christianity*.

For example, Charles Fillmore, one of the founders of the Unity School, taught, "God is not loving....God does not love anybody or anything. God is the love *in* everybody and everything. God is love...God exercises none of his attributes except through the inner consciousness of the universe and man."[3] Most Hindus would come much nearer endorsing the statement above than would most Christians.

Under the label of being Christian, such groups as *Christian* Science and the Unity School of *Christianity* are movements which have helped to popularize Eastern ideas in the Western world.

4) *Religious agnosticism....*

The influence of the scientific method in the search for truth has greatly affected the quest for religious truth in the past generation. In the resultant popular mind, "truth" in religion is difficult to "prove" with test tubes and lab experiments. Therefore, there has emerged what might be labeled "agnosticism", that is, the idea that religious truth cannot be known for sure. So, many persons have concluded that there are no *absolutes* in religion. Therefore, some persons reason that one religion is as good as another. In the secular world, religious truth is often said to be "relative", that is, not absolutely certain. This is the result of a scientific age which forces its definition of truth on all realms of thinking. Religious truth has been caught in

---

[3]Charles Fillmore, *Jesus Christ Heals*, (Unity Village: Unity Publishing Trust) p. 27

this trap. Eastern religions have come to this age at an opportune time of indiscriminate acceptance of all religious truths as tentative.

5) *Meditation....*

More than 1,000,000 Americans have paid fees ranging from $100 to $125 to be trained in meditation. One Zen monastery in California regularly has more than one hundred students per weekend for their introduction to the practice of meditation.

In a stress-filled era in which many persons seek a temporary escape from a nerve-shattering world, medittion has an immediate appeal. Most Christians, whether Protestant or Catholic, have a long heritage of emphasis on personal piety. Eastern religions such as Zen have found a ready acceptance from those who need or desire inner peace.

6) *Search for the bizarre....*

There is no doubt that some participation in Buddhism or the rituals of Americanized gurus is due to efforts by American youth to shock their American Christian parents. Christian missionaries in Japan report that a Japanese youth who want to shock their Shinto-Buddhist parents will become a Lutheran. In America, the reverse happens. A shaved head will usually achieve the desired result of shock.

7) *World-consciousness....*

The world is shrinking in the sense that instant communication and faster transportation have made each person indeed a "world citizen." A flood in Tokyo affects those who live in Tucamcari. There has developed a "togetherness" in despair as well as in joy as this generation is made aware than one society's problems are part of a total picture of a world community.

As a result, some people are attracted toward the Eastern religions because they are symbols of being a world citizen, aware of the Oriental and Asian world. In this first generation of expanse to a universal communications explosion, some persons have responded favorably to the call of the Moslem minaret or the mystery of the Zen Roshi (master).

8) *Idealism....*

Some of the world religions make an appeal to such ideals as "universal love" as an over-riding theme. They stress that love and acceptance are the only roads to world peace and brotherhood. For example, the Bahai World Faith adherents suggest two prime goals when making an appeal for new converts: universal peace and universal brotherhood. They call for a unity of religions and governments.

American youth speak of a "performance gap" in which adult Christians talk more about love than they practice it.

This is at times done out of naivete, in the assumption that all religious traditions teach the same definitions of such words as "love." There is, however, a sharp contrast between Buddhist metta (empathy) and Christian agape' (love in action). The growth of idealistic Eastern religions is due to the mixture of failing to define terms and the aforementioned "performance gap."

9) *Existentialism....*

A popular strand of thought within existentialism asks two key question, "Does it feel good?" and "Will it work?" Celebration, awareness and search for practical happiness permeate the standards of those influenced by popular existentialism. This has added to the development of such phrases as, "Whatever turns you on" and "Different strokes for different folks." The Eastern forms of religion have profited from this existentialist emphasis on practical celebration.

10) *Internationals....*

There is a growing number of International students and residents here in the United States. They bring their religious rituals and ideas with them. As Americans become their friends, they come to appreciate the values of their new-found friends.

East has met West with remarkable speed and receptivity. Phenomenology, with its multifaced spotlight, helps the student to see some of the reasons why this is the case. No other method will suffice to offer a thorough analysis, because no other method analyses from so many perspectives. This method will be used throughout this book. Each chapter will combine insights from history, anthropology, psychology, sociology, economics, politics, philosophy and other disciplines as they apply.

The study of religion is an exciting adventure, combining self-realization with social awareness and potential improved spiritual growth. The rewards are worth the cost. Let's get going!

BIBLIOGRAPHY

Norman Anderson, *The World's Religions* (Grand Rapids: Eerdmans, 1950)

Geoffrey Parrinder, *The Faiths of Mankind* (New York: Thomas Y. Crowell Co., 1964)

Chapter I

Ancient Religions

"Ancient Religions" is a phrase used in this chapter to denote a time period of about 3000-1500 BC. Prior to that time, humans were unable to write and leave records, at least as far as archeologists today are able to determine. After 2000 BC, some of the major world religions begin to develop, such as Judaism.

As far as scholars can tell, the first writing was invented and put into popular use in Sumeria, "the land between the rivers," i.e., the Tigris and Euphrates. Today this area is called Iraq, lying at the Eastern tip of the "Fertile Crescent." Sumeria is chosen for presentation in this chapter because it was the background for the invention of writing and because Sumeria was the approximate location of the Ur of the Chaldees, from which came one Abraham. It is Abraham to whom Jews, Moslems and Christians alike look for inspiration.

All ancient religious forms, whether it be in Sumeria or Greece or Rome or Egypt, has six characteristics in common. They were:

1) *A creation myth*

Here the word myth is not used in the sense of a "fairy tale" which may not have historical facts at its base. The word "myth" here is historical saga used as a narrative vehicle designed to impart deep philosophical, moral and theological insights. Such an example is Genesis 1 and 2 in the Hebrew Scriptures. The recitation of the concept of man being made of dirt has deep significance for he Hebrews, Christians and Moslems of today. All the ancient religions had their creation myth or myths.

2) *Animism*

Permeating each of the ancient religions was an emphasis on spirits, powers and beings which brought good or evil to the people. Taboo was common, in which it was thought that some beings may have too much power. All ancient religions had the reality of power which permeated all of life, but some beings or objects more than others. (See chapter on Animism.)

3) *Gods*

Multiple deities were common to all the ancient religions. They were usually fertility gods and goddesses related to the agricultural needs of the people. They may also have been personifications of nature's strongest elements, such as the sun and moon or thunder and lightening. No ancient religion was devoid of its deities.

4) *Relation to nature*

It was through the deities usually that persons involved in the ancient religions sought to relate in a positive manner to nature. The heavens, especially the tracking of the stars and planets, was important also. This led to the art of astrology as a central part of all the ancient religions. The Eastern magi who came to see the child Jesus were but one example of such interest.

5) *Relation to the ruler*

Ancient religious life was greatly affected by their way of viewing the ruler in charge. At times he was seen as divine and eternal. It is common, especially in Egypt, to record that a particular leader lived thousands of years. This was their way of saying that he was a gracious and powerful ruler. At times the ruler demanded and got sacrifices. Elaborate funerals were planned and executed by priests at the death of a ruler.

6) *Afterlife*

Each of the ancient religions had a predominant view of the afterlife. For example, the Hebrews had Sheol, a damp, cold place in which persons lived as shadows. Sheol was the common lot of all who died. Persons being affected by these views of the afterlife were common in the ancient religions.

Around 1900 BC, Abraham was born in Sumeria. By this time, the Sumerians were already an advanced civilization. For more than a thousand years they had had a king. They were highly successful in art, trade and agriculture. There was a network of irrigation canals. Sumerian craftsmen, in Abraham's day, were already doing exquisite work in gold, silver and other metals.

Religion was, about 2000 BC, at the very heart of Sumerian life. The priests who cared for the temples were also the scholars, teachers and physicians for the people. The priests also functioned as the official historians and scribes copying sacred literature for the nation.

Sumeria was open on all sides to the invasion of both armies and whole cultures. About 2500 BC, small city-states began to appear in Sumeria. Their respective ideologies were built on localized animism and accompanying gods. The *Zi*, or spirits, were viewed as real and generally feared. The names changed from locale to locale, but the phenomenon remained the same.

An early development were Triads of gods, especially among the priests in the larger temples. One of the earliest of these was Anu, Enlil and Ea. Ea was the god of all waters, both on and below the earth. Enlil was the god of the earth and the atmosphere just above it. Anu was the patron god of the powerful city-state of Uruk and was the god of the heavens. So, there was a three-layered view of the earth with a deity for each level in ancient Sumeria.

Enlil was probably the successor to an ancient Sumerian god, Enki. A hymn to Enlil emerged. It reads, in part:

> I am the 'great Storm' which
> goes forth out of the 'great
> below'!
> I am the lord of the land.
> I am the 'big brother' of
> the gods.
> I am he who brings full prosperity

I am the record keeper of
    heaven and earth.
I am the ear and mind of the
    lands.
I am the lord, I am one whose
    command is unquestioned...

A second Triad of gods which emerged in ancient Sumeria was composed of Sin, Shamash and Ishtar.

When a city the size and power of Babylon or Nineveh became powerful enough to conquer other city-states, that event was recorded with flourish in the theology of the cities. In those records, the gods of the conqueror are pictured as overcoming those of the conquered peoples. It is by this method that such deities as Marduk and Ishtar came to achieve status.

Ishtar (from whence came Esther in the Hebrew Scriptures and Easter in modern Christendom) was the goddess of generation and ferility, therefore, the goddess of love and sex. The earliest of the Sumerian fertility cults centered around Ishtar.

An ancient Summerian myth tells the story of Ishtar living in a type of paradise named Dilmun. All there was pure and clean. There was no pain or sorrow or old age. Yet, there was one thing lacking. There was no fresh water. Ishtar went into a rage and insisted that Enlil get the sun god, Anu, to supply fresh water in abundance. Enlil went out in search of Anu. Along the way he got sexually side-tracked and impregnated three maidens representative of three successive generations. When he returned, Ishtar refused to look at him. There was now no joy in Dilmun. Ishtar and Enlil were engaged thereafter in a running battle.

The implications of this Sumerian myth are significant for the everyday life of the people. If the fertility goddess is in conflict with the god of the earth and atmosphere, the farmer is caught in a constant struggle to try to unite the two. Much of ancient Sumerian ritual was designed to do just that.

Marduk was another key god in ancient Sumeria. He was the son of Ea, the god of the waters. According to the creation myth of the Mesopatamians, it was Marduk who fought Tiamat in a struggle for the control of the cosmos. Marduk defeated Tiamat after a long struggle. He then split the two halves of her body, thereby forming heaven and earth.

It is 'Enuma Elish', recorded about 1800 BC, which tells of the struggle between Marduk and Tiamat. It is so named for the first two words of the document, which translated mean, ''When on high.'' After Marduk defeats Tiamat, the document concludes as the other gods build a temple for Marduk. It reads, in part:

You, Marduk, are the most
    honored of the great gods...
We have granted you Kingship
    over the great universe.

When you sit in the Assembly,
your word shall be supreme.
Your weapons shall not fail
They shall swish your foes!

Ishtar lives on in the 'Enuma Elish' in the myth concerning her descent into the underworld. She is in search for her lover, Tammuz. This is typical of a poetic account of the continuing life-death cycle throughout the Mesopatamian area. As the story goes, Ishtar with great courage makes her way down into the dark and filthy regions. There she faces her sister, the cruel queen of the domain without hope. She brings back Tammuz, her lover, from it. When Tammuz rises from the dead, there is great hope because life and joy have returned to the world.

Beside myth, which gave the Sumerians mixed feelings toward gods and goddesses of fertility, the peoples of ancient Mesopotamia had certain methods designed to placate those deities or live in harmony with them.

One method was divination, or foretelling the future. One popular method of seeing into the future was Hepatoscopy, the "reading" of a sheep's liver.

Astrology was well developed in ancient Sumeria. The dominant god of astrology was Sin, the moon god, also known as the lord of wisdom. Astrology emerged into a courtly pursuit and helped rulers determine how to govern the important matters of state. When the common people understood that they could not use astrology without intricate training, they turned to dream interpretations, omens and ordeals.

Part of this interest in divination and astrology was caused by an emerging interest in the future, especially determining elements of the afterlife. Originally death was seen as the end in Mesopotamia. However, thoughtful persons began to yearn for a better explanation of the afterlife. As a planet, the *Gilgamesh Epic* emerged. As the story goes, Gilgamesh left the throne of godhood to go in search of life in the hereafter. He had to overcome ferocious beasts. Then Gilgamesh discovered that the magic plant of immortality grows at the bottom of the sea. So, Gilgamesh weighted himself with stones and went to the bottom of the sea. There he got the magic plant. Alas, on his way home a serpent stole the plant. So, Gilgamesh, the frustated hero, returns home without the key to immortality for all the people. A chapter near the end of the myth reads in part:

Gilgamesh saw a well whose
water was cool.
He went down into it to bathe
in the water
A serpent snuffed the fragrance
of the plant....
Thereupon Gilgamesh sits and
weeps,
His tears running down over
his face....

14

As a result of this negative epic, the Mesopatamian people continued to face a horrible existence beyond death. The world of the dead was pictured as an existence with nothing to do and no pleasure to enjoy. The place itself was pictured as dusty, cold and dark. The ancient Hebrews reflected the fact that their father came from the Ur of the Chaldees as they formulated a similiar picture of Sheol.

The burial rites of the Mesopatamians show that the dead seem to have been considered as a continuing part of the family. It was the custom to bury the dead under the house where the rest the family lived. After a few generations, it was common for the family graves under the house to be so many that the house was abandoned to those dead and another was built. In the Ur of about 2600 BC, ''death pits'' of kings have been unearthed containing almost eighty bodies of persons who died with the king as willing eternal servants. This was done because the servants believed that they would join the king as gods in the afterlife. So, the common people were afforded immortality directly in proportion to the amount and quality of contact they had with the ruler.

The most remarkable piece of Sumerian mythology, because of its implications for modern Bible study, is the ancient myth of the great flood. It seems, according to the myth, when the Sumerian gods decided to destroy all mankind with a flood, a friendly god warned the saintly Ziusudra to build himself a ship. In his obedience he survived and also saved the seed of mankind and other forms of life. When the flood subsided, Ziusudra offered sacrifices to the many gods. They then permitted him to dwell with them in the paradise called Dilmun.

The Akkadian version of the same story is derived from the long *Gilgamesh Epic*. In the flood portion of that epic, Gilgamesh, the hero, hears the story from Utnapishtim. Utnapishtim says that he built a great ship to escape the flood which covered an important city. He, like Ziusudra, was given immortality because he sacrificed to the gods after the flood to show his thankfulness.

The story reads, in part:

Aboard the ship take thou
    the seed of all living
    things
The ship which thou shalt
    build
Her dimensions shall be to
    measure.
Equal shall be her width and
    her length....

When the seventh day arrived
I sent forth and set free a
    dove.
The dove went forth but
    came back
There was no resting place
    for it and she turned
    around....

Thereupon Enlil went aboard
  the ship
Holding me by the hand, he
  took me aboard
He took my wife aboard and
  made her kneel by my side.
Standing between us, he
  touched our foreheads to
  bless us:
Hitherto Utnapishtim has
  been but human
Henceforth Utnapishtim and
  his wife shall be like
  unto gods....

It is apparent that these two epics, Sumerian and Akkadian, differ radically from the Biblical account. The point of the two earlier stories is that the hero becomes a god. Noah, in the Hebrew Scriptures, is embarrassed in nakedness and drunkenness.

Conclusion....
The ancient religions still live, particularly the Sumerian types. They live through apparent modern parallels and by being the base for modern religious movements. When humans first came into existence, they were religious beings. The Sumerian invention of writing affords us with the earliest written records to document that religiosity. Whenever one reads of Abraham of appeals to his daily horoscope for guidance, he stands in direct indebtedness to the Sumerians.

BIBLIOGRAPHY

H. Breasted, *Development of Religion and Thought in Ancient Egypt* (New York: Harper and Row, 1959)
Edwin Oliver James, *Prehistoric Religion* (London: Thames and Hudson, 1957)
Johannes Maringer, *The Gods of Prehistoric Man* (New York: Alfred A. Knopf, Inc., 1960)
Alexander Marshack, *The Roots of Civilization* (New York: McGraw Hill Book, Co., 1972)
Isaac Mendelsohn, *Religions of the Ancient Near East* (New York: The Liberal Arts Press, Inc., 1955)

Marduk:

Hello, my name is Marduk. I lived as a trader in the days of the man you call Abraham. Why he would have ever wanted to leave Ur, I cannot understand. Ours was a very advanced civilization, profiting from being on the Fertile Crescent, a trade route leading to the best markets of the known world. Maybe it was from one of the caravan leaders that Abraham heard of Yahweh and a land to be given him. He could have stayed here, we certainly have plenty of gods to choose from. As a matter of fact, I am named for one of them.

According to a sheep's liver reading done at my birth, I am supposed to be brave like Marduk. Before I start on a journey I am sure that all the gods are pleased so that the gods will watch over my household while I am gone. Our gods helped make us a superior people. It was our writing that allowed us to keep accurate records This kept us from being cheated by other such inferior peoples as the Hapiru.

Enlilia:

Hello, my name is Enlilia. Welcome to the year you called 2020 BC. I am a priest in the Holy Temple of Enlil located in Haran. It is my duty to offer daily sacrifices and prayers to Enlil. It is he who guarantees great crops for my people. I was trained for three years in the daily ritual of the temple before I was ever allowed to offer a sacrifice. It is important that the ceremonies be ritually correct so as to please Enlil. Should he become angry, our crops could be scorched.

We are required to know the paths of the stars as well. I was born under a good sign for becoming a priest. Perhaps this is why I may be chief priest for Enlil in all of Haran within a few years. Luckily, we have taken astrology from the hands of the illiterate people, for they were misusing it. We priests are the ones called to keep the ritual pure. Excuse me, please. My elder is calling. It is time for our daily sacrifice at high noon.

Chapter II
Animism

During the past century, an early scholar in the field of sociology and anthropology toured the world and made observations about what he considered as "primitive" religions. His name was Sir Edward Burnett Tylor and it was he who gave to religious study the term "animism." He observed that religion as he was it had one element in common. That was a power he called "anima" and he noted that the "Aboriginals" saw it as a power inhabitating every living thing. Some beings had more of this powerful substance than did others, according to Tylor. Some accumulated so much of it as to be dangerous, or TABOO.

It was Sir Tylor who did early research on animism,[1] but further study has shown that the world he knew on the surface is far from complicated than he imagined.

Religions which appear "primitive" to those with more organized ritual and monotheistic theologies are complex. Amidst the complexities, however, there are some elements. They are:

1) A holistic view of all life. For the Animist, all of life is a whole. Every activity from birth to death is interpreted as belonging to a religious whole. In fact, all of life is religious. There is no separation between the sacred and the secular. There is the strong fact also among the animistic peoples; i.e., no one of the individual parts of a society can be analyzed apart from the other parts.

2) Spiritual forces are vital and permeating all of life. All the universe throbs with sacred forces. Events in life such as accidents or unexpected good fortune are the result of Spirit forces at work in the midst of those events.

3) Myths. These are ancient stories retold countless times during each generation to remind the people of their roots and to suggest ways of pleasing the spirits.

4) Rituals. These are especially true in animistic societies during times of important passeges in life, such as birth, puberty and marriage. Ritual also permeates trivial everyday activity as well. Such events as eating and cooking are carried out in a ritualistic fashion.

5) Rhythm. Seasons and the growing of crops are done in proper sequence in animistic society. There are times when things are "right" or "wrong" which the outsider may not be able to judge accurately. Time is counted in events which occur according to a

---

[1]See: Sir Edward Burnett Tylor, *Religion in Primitive Culture* Volume II, (New York: Harper Publishers, 1958)

rhythm, not in the mere counting off of seconds and minutes. Most cultures in the world do not even have words for "seconds" and "minutes." Rituals help in maintaining rhythm and animistic priests must know when as well as how to perform rites.

Managing anima....

The animist, in order to co-exist with the numerous spirits which rule his world, must learn to handle them in such a way as to steer clear of danger and manipulate these spirits to work for him. There are many effective means for doing these tasks. Among the most used in the animist world are:

1) *Words*

They may be used to make crops grow or ward off evil. In general, words are used to control some inherent anima in an object. On occasion, words may constitute power within themselves. Words are viewed as dangerous forces in most animistic societies. If one speaks of the death of a friend and that friend dies soon thereafter, the speaker may be charged with murder in some animistic groups.

Words may also be used to utter beautiful prayers. One example is:

Great Spirit!
Piler up of rocks into tower-
    ing mountains:
When thou stampest on the
    stone,
The dust rises and fills the
    land.
Hardness of the precipice;
Waters of the pool turn
Into misty rain when stirred.
Vessel overflowing with oil!
Father of Runji,
Who seweth the heavens like
    cloth;
Let him knit together that
    which is below.
Caller forth of the branching
    trees:
Thou bringeth forth the shoots
That they stand erect.
Thou hast filled the land with
    mankind,
The dust rises on high, O Lord![2]

2) *Sacrifices*

Sacrifices are used by the animists as a way of bringing gifts to the gods. Since the gods cannot receive the gifts by reaching out to take them, the gifts must be changed in form. Burning or rotting is

---

[2]E. G. Parrinder, *African Ideas of God* (London: Lutterworth Press, 1962) p. 127

sometimes used. At times, food sacrifices are made to the gods. After a few hours, the priest announces to the participants that the essence of the food has been consumed. Frequently the "food of the gods" is then consumed by the animists with such mutual side benefits as virility and long life resulting.

3) *Taboos*

The animist is always careful not to offend a god. One way to do this is not to come near any object with too much anima. One example is found in the Hebrew Scriptures. In the process of transporting the ark, it fell off the beast of burden and burst. When some men accidently looked at it, they were struck dead on the spot.

4) *Religious specialists.*

In animistic societies, there are two dominant types of religious persons. They are the priest and the shaman.

The priest is viewed as the mediator standing between the people and their gods. Becoming a priest is no easy matter in most animistic societies. For example, among the Ashanti in west Africa, there is a three-year training program involved. The first year is mainly a process of being purified. The second year is given to the study of laws, mores and taboos. The final year is given to perfecting ceremonial rites.

The shaman has an even broader range of responsibilities. He is expected to be a healer, a diviner of the future and a placater of the angry gods. In the process of healing, for example, he is often the diagnostician, prescriber of herbs and enemy of evil spirits.

Basic beliefs....

1) *A Supreme Being*

In spite of the fact that the animist has many gods, he usually has a Supreme Being. Usually he is a sky god who is viewed as Creator and sustainer of the universe.

2) *Spirits*

The animist has extreme difficulty in separating deities and spirits. Frequently the spirits are seen as the "living dead." They dwell in trees, rocks, caves or animals. They are quite unpredictable and people are careful not to offend them. Small offerings of food are often left near the dwelling places.

There is a common belief among animists that a person once dead dwells both in the "Land of the Dead" and here on earth. This makes funeral rites most important. The proper rites speed the soul on to the "Land of the Dead" and serve as a guarantee that they will not return often to plague the living.

3) *Sin and morality*

Good and evil within an animistic society are judged by a simple standard, i.e., whether it does harm to the well-being of the society. For example, the Sewang peoples of Malaysia believe that their god, Karei, allows them to kill a man not of their own tribe.

These beliefs hold the animistic societies together, even in a rudimentary type of theological creed.

Magic....

Magic is central to the practice of animism. It can be used to secure good or to produce harm. That which produces good is called "white" and that designed to work evil is called "black" even though there are very few witches who would do either good or evil consistently. Therefore, most witches would be what the animist calls "grey" witches: those who do both good and evil on occasion.

Magic is usually based on contact or association. If a person deeming himself a witch, for example, is asked to cast an evil spell on a person, he may ask for an object that belongs to that person. There is also magic by association in which the witch may perform an act related to the desired result. For example, persons in pre-Castro Cuba frequently would have a pregnant woman plant the seeds for everyone's crop.

Magic is sometimes used for purposes of divining the future. Dreams, birds' flights, or the pattern of a column of smoke may be read. Usually the client wants to know the cause of a calamity, the nature of a future endeavor or what is going on some distance away.

Magic is sometimes used to determine guilt or innocence by the use of ordeals. The accused or some member of his immediate family is forced to a potentially dangerous test. If he survives without injury, the accused is deemed innocent.

In the hills of Laos, if one accuses another of being an evil witch, both are placed in a pot of boiling oil. The first one to jump out is believed guiltly and is clubbed to death by the villagers.

The Ainus....

An example of a living animistic people are the Ainu of Japan. They view themselves as the original people of Japan.

The Ainu have gods and goddesses of vegetation, of water and of the heavenly bodies. The fire god is important and is worshipped over the open hearth. The Supreme god is called Pase Kamui, or the "God over all."

The common fetishes among the Ainu are called Inao and are carved from wood. The word Inao means "message bearer". There is a common household fetish made of lilac wood and called the "ancestral caretaker."

Cereal-worship is central to the Ainu religion. At harvest time there are cereal offerings made to the grain itself.

The bear festival is fascinating, but cruel. A bear, captured as a cub, is nurtured until it is a year old and fat. The bear is subjected to torture with blunt arrows. When the bear is thoroughly enraged and the young braves are in a frenzy of excitement, they rush in and kill the bear with a knife. The blood is carefully caught and drunk by some of the men while it is still warm. The bear is then skinned and beheaded. Offerings of food are made to the bear's head. After the bear's flesh is ready for eating, some of his own meat and raw blood are offered to the head for eating. After the bear's head has had time to eat, a banquet is held. The feast ends with the bear's head erected on a totem pole. In this way, it is believed by the Ainu that the gods will feed the group for another year.

The modern Animist....

Traditional animism permeates much of today's world, in such places as the "out back" in Australia, the hills of South America and Pacific Islands. However, the modern sophisticated American has been called animist at heart.

The presence of 75,000 full-time witches in the America of the late 1970's is but one example of the animism which lies beneath the surface of the "modern." Halloween is a classic example. In the annual reenactment of this Old Religion (the animistic system which predominated in northern Europe from the 6th through the 14th centuries AD) festival, the American public has jack-o-lanterns mindful of the burning stubble on the fields of England six centuries ago. By the light of those fires, spirits could come up out of the graves and demand a meal. If this demand was unmet, the spirit could take a household member back to the grave with him. Ever go trick or treating? With a mask? In the "modern" world?

Conclusion....

The animist lives in constant interaction with his world and his gods. He is never free to have a moment unrelated to religion. His spirit is as much alive in the tatooed bush dweller in New Guinea as the tatooed sailor in San Diego.

BIBLIOGRAPHY

Edwin A. Burtt, *Man Seeks the Divine* (New York: Harper and Brothers, 1957)
Carl Etter, *Ainu Life and Folklore* (Chicago: Wilcox and Follett Co., 1949)
E.O. James, *Prehistoric Religion* (New York: Barnes and Noble, 1961)
Geoffrey Parrinder, *African Traditional Religion* (New York: Hutchinson's University Library, 1954)
Elman Rogers Service, *Profile of Primitive Cultures* (New York: Harper and Brothers, 1958)

Etim:

My name is Etim. I live in a sparsely populated part of Nigeria. I am twenty-nine years old and am known among my people as a healer, although in America you might call me a "witch doctor."

For five years I trained to be doing what I do. From my birth I have been said to have what you might call "psychic" gifts. When I was five, I could remember back beyond my mother's womb. As a teenager, some of my clan noted that I could predict such future events as the death of a relative.

The biggest event that has happened around here in a generation was last year's installation of our new king. The king is viewed as being given eternal life. It was my job to grow a goat and keep him pure for a year. The king was given immortality by the eating of the meat and broth of that goat. The king was pleased and has asked that I take part in the annual renewal festival. The gods are pleased.

Cassandra:

My new witch name is Cassandra. I am a twenty-eight-year-old psychiatric nurse and I live in Little Rock. My new religion is the Old Religion and I am a practicing witch. Please don't picture me as a fly-by-night woman dressed in black on a broomstick. I am a legitimate practitioner of my religion and should be classified along with priests, ministers and rabbis.

My potions and incantations are all part of my ritualistic paraphanelia. When my coven meets, I am in my role as priest. It feels good to be a part of an ancient religion.

Witchcraft is also helpful on other occasions. The other day a thief broke into our home and stole some items. I knew immediately that I should put some hog fat and salt on the open hearth. It works....

Chapter III
African Religions

Africa never deserved to be called the "dark" continent. It was stuck with that label by European and American travelers there who could not seem to grasp the complexity of life in Africa. Africa has become the focal point of social upheaval in the past generation as millions struggle for freedom from outside domination.

The student who still thinks of "natives" roaming through "jungles" in search of heads was always only partially correct. Today such images are even less accurate. Modern cities dot the vast African continent, based on developed economics.

A few facts about the African continent are pertinent to this chapter. As a continent, Africa has three times the land mass of the United States. One-third of the quarter billion residents of Africa live in Nigeria. Africa is as varied as it is vast. The desert bedouin of Morocco has little in common with the Afrikaner of South Africa or the bushmen of Tanzania. Yet, many Americans still think of Africa as one nation. Elementary school textbooks still have units on Japan, Mexico and Africa, as if the African continent were one nation. There are more than fifty nations in modern Africa. The image of "wild animals" still dominates some American images of Africa. Most Africans have never seen a lion, except perhaps in a zoo.

The study of African religions is so new in any depth that one occasionally still runs across terms such as "superstition," "primitive," "supernatural," "tribe" and "ignorant savages" even among reputable scholars. These terms were prevalent among reputable sociologists a century ago. Further investigation has shown them to be premature labels with little substance.

Modern Africa is the home for many religions. Estimates vary, but approximately thirty per cent of the peoples of Africa are Moslem, thirty per cent Christian and thirty per cent involved in indigenous forms of religious expression. The other ten per cent are Hindu, Bahai, Sikhs, Jains or Buddhist, primarily in East Africa. Of course, such divisions are arbitrary since many who are Christians still practice indigenous rites, especially in emergencies. The same is true with nominal Moslems. It is primarily with the indigenous religions of Africa that this chapter is concerned. This is done in seven categories: religion as social reform, ethics, religious "holy men," ritual, man, myths and the afterlife.

Religion as social reform....

Early African response to colonial rule was largely peaceful submission. There were, early and late, however, some rebellious uprisings. Most of these had religious stimuli. Even in 1978, it is three Protestant-trained revolutionaries who are leading black groups in revolt against domination by white in South Africa.

A classic example was Kinjikitile and his revolt against colonial rule in 1905-07 in German East Africa, today known as Tanzania. Kinjikitile announced that he was possessed by "the Hongo spirit sent upon him by his superior, Bokero." This allowed him to be a social prophet with a wide appeal across clan groups.

His reputation soon spread as he promised holy water as a protection against injury in battle. Some of his lieutenants grew impatient and revolted against the German cotton growers before Kinjikitile was ready. As a result, he was seized and hanged. Seventy-five thousands of his followers died in the premature uprising.

Although the revolt was unsuccessful in removing German colonial control, it was successful in arousing organizational revolt. This is but one example of the manner in which indigenous religions have been used as background for social protest. This picture is far removed from the image of "witch doctor" in the bush offering isolated cures.

Man....

In general, African indigenous religions tend to define man in terms of the social group or groups to which he belongs, not as an isolated individual.

The Yoruba peoples are an example of this social identity. The Yoruba think of man as having multiple souls, each representing a separate dimension within the society.

It is held by the Yoruba that before a person is born, his fate is largely decided. His occupation, successes or failures, and the time of death are already set. The high god, Olorun, makes this known to the affected person through an "ori," or intermediary. So, the ori becomes the key to personal success and failure. It is a prime purpose in life to keep the ori happy. This is stated in this verse:

It is the ori that guides,
That we wear the crown of
    money.
It is the ori that guides
That we walk with the royal
    stick of heads....
Oh, hail Ori.[1]

As the Yoruba views life, it is on a balanced scale. It is ordained and conditioned by group identity, yet it is related to personal freedom in the development of one's character, provided that the ori is pleased.

---

[1]Samuel Oyruloye Abogunrin, "Man in Yoruba Thought," (Bachelor of Arts Thesis, Department of Religious Studies and Philosophy, Univ. of Ibadan, 1972), p. 45.

Each person is to find his own lot in life, guided somewhat by his predetermined destiny and responsible to the mores of his society in which he finds his basic identity.

Religious "holy men"....

In most African societies, there are three basic types of holy men. They are priests, prophets and diviners.

The priest is primarily a mediator between the people and their gods. His chief mark is elaborate ritual.

An example of a priestly role is that among the Dogan peoples. A Hogan is the title given a Dogan. He functions as the head of a council of elders who represent Dogan ancestors. The Hogan is seen as representing the entire universe, as he unites himself to the social, agricultural and cosmic orders at various times and through various rituals.

Among the Dogan there is the Lebe, viewed as the ancestor who sustains life on earth. The reincarnated Lebe, in the form of a serpent, comes to the Hogan every night to lick his body and give him the power to function as the Hogan for another day.

The Hogan so regulates his daily activity as to flow with the rhythm of nature. At dawn he rises facing east. By his daily and seasonal movements, he helps to regulate and reflect the cosmic forces. Thus gives to the Dogan land and people their fertility. It is the Hogan who functions as priest, mediating between the persons of Dogan.

"Prophets" also appear among the African indigenous religions. As with Amos in the Hebrew Scriptures, it is the role of the prophet to make judgments and stimulate action resulting in social justice. They may, therefore, become the focus of major social protest movements, as in the case of Kinjikitile mentioned earlier. The prophets charismatic leadership can inspire thousands to seek equality with vigor that can only be divinely-based. On occasion, the prophet may announce that he not only *represents* deity, he is indeed possessed completely by a god. Therefore, it is not him speaking, but the god speaking through him. So, success in a social protest movements is not usually judged by whether the desired social changes took place, but whether the prophet spoke accurately for the gods.

Diviners....

The diviners are concerned with helping the people in the African indigenous religions have access to knowledge beyond normal space and time limitations. The "diviner" may predict the future or tell the client what is going on miles away.

The Yoruba peoples call their diviner a "babalawo" or "father of secrets." It is held that one is chosen from birth to be a babalawo. Often more then ten years is spent in study under a master babalawo.

When the diviner is consulted, he frequently gives his answer about the future in a series of poems. After hearing these, the client chooses the one he considers most applicable to his situation. After choosing his poem, the client pays or thanks the "father of secrets" and departs. When he is home, he performs the prescribed rituals or actions so as to get the desired results. The Yoruba are but one example of a group seeking "diviners" to give some assurance about the future.

Rituals....

Ritual is the backbone of the living entity called African indigenous religions. The ritual is designed to so communicate with the gods as to change the human situation for the better or to maintain the status quo if it seen as healthy.

Ritual is frequently built around "rites of passage," that is, key transitional movements in life.

If the ritual is performed properly by the priest, the next stage in life will be a happy one. If not, let the client beware!

A key "rite of passage" is that concerned with puberty. Among the Bambara of Mali, the crossing-over of boys into manhood takes several years and six indentifiable stages. The last stage is called kore. The theme of this last stage is rebirth through the acquiring of knowledge. This is done at the initiation grove, located near the village. Mothers may come near the grove and bring food to their sons, but they may not look upon them during this time.

The chief audio-visual aid in obtaining the desired knowledge is the Kalani, a long pole on which are hung 250 objects representative of all things within their universe. The boys must memorize the symbolic meaning of all of these objects. For example, an arrow may represent war of hunting. Having learned that life's simple things symbolize profound truths, the boys re-enter the village as men fully aware and enlightened. They know now that they are part of an enlightened family.

This ritual must be carried out correctly or the Bambara boys enter manhood with one or more curses upon them.

Ethics....

According to many of the creation myths of the African indigenous religions, man was originally created in a state of happiness and childlike ignorance. God had also provided him with all the necessities of life, either directly or accessible through man's innate powers. So, man originally lived in a state of paradise. In that situation, the High God gave man certain commandments to follow. So long as man kept these rules, his relationship to God was a healthy one. But, in most African mythology, this relationship was disrupted.

According to the Ashanti peoples, God originally lived in the sky just above mankind. However, the mother of all men constantly distrubed God by making corn on her pestle. So, God moved up a little higher. The woman, desiring to be closer to God, ordered her sons to build a structure from mortars to reach God. They were but one mortar short. The mother ordered the sons to take the bottom mortar and place it on top of the mortar. When they did so, the whole structure collapsed. The survivors gave up the idea of following God by building structures. The result was separation.

28

Since man is basically separated from God, the role of the ritual and other paraphernalia of the African indigenous religions is designed to placate or please those gods so alienated. This makes the role of the mediator especially important. Hence, the numerous priests in African religious forms.

Myths....

In African mythology, there is much of what westerners would call history. Oral traditions prove amazingly accurate when presenting those past events which mould everyday African life.

For example, the Shilluk peoples of southern Sudan have an impressive set of traditions centered around their divine kings. Shilluks tell that their history began with the wanderings of Nyikang, their founder-hero. Nyikang was born into a paradise far to the south of modern Sudan. However, Nyikang quarreled with his brother over the possession of that paradise. Nyikang lost and was banished.

When Nyikang came to the Sudan, he conquered the inhabitants of the land, descendants of the Sun. The Sun was driven back to the sky.

Today the Shilluk kings are still regarded as defenders of the land from foreign enemies. He is united with the supreme god, Juok, in that task. One poem states:

Nyikang is the Father of
the Shilluk
And he has united with Juok,
Who rules the world.
Nyikang himself wants the
battle against the foreigners.[2]

This myth serves to tie the Shilluks to their history. This provides continuity with the past and a reference point for planning their future.

The afterlife ....

Most African peoples, like the Hebrews, have mythological explanations for how death came into the world. Currently, death is usually viewed as a direct result of sorcery. In spite of this, death is seen by most African peoples as a continuation, not a complete cessation of existence. The spirit simply moves on to another level of existence.

Burial is the most common method of dealing with the dead. In many African societies, it is the custom to bury along with the body such items as food and weapons.

The status of the recently deceased is an enigma to most Africans. He is usually regarded as part of the "living dead," i.e., he is neither alive physically nor dead relative to having access to his former family and clan.

---

[2]Wilhelm Hofmayr, *Die Shilluk* (Vienna: Administration des Anthropos, 1926), p. 421.

The next world is viewed by most African peoples as being geographically "here," i.e., not separated by distance. A number of peoples, including the Yoruba, believe that at death the personality of the deceased person goes to the sky to be with God. This, however, does not cut them off from their own human family. For the majority of African societies, the hereafter is but a continuation of life. This means that social status is retained. As soon as a person dies, he becomes a "living dead." He retains his given name. When he appears in a vision to family members, they recognize him. Family members perform ritual to aid him in the hereafter. He must be cared for in that new state.

These seven elements make it clear that the indigenous people of Africa have complex views of God, self and society. Further study will serve to demonstrate that complexity.

The Dahomey....

Eugene A. Nida presents the Dahomey of West Africa as a living example of African indigenous religions. He says:

Dahomean religion has a pantheon to rival the ancient Greeks...The average Dahomean is not quite sure just how many souls he has, although he knows very well that he has more than one....When a Dahomean dies, his personal soul, which is described as his voice or personality, is believed to take a trip to the land of the dead....Once in the world of dead souls, a new soul joins his relatives who preceded him there....

Dahomeans are well endowed with gods....One group of Dahomean gods consists of the sky deities....The other pantheons of Dahomean gods are the earth gods and the thunder gods....In addition to the gods, Dahomeans also believe in other kinds of spirits that are worshiped and feared in varying degrees....Dahomean society is divided into thirty-nine or more groupings based on actual or imaginary family relationships....Each of these Dahomean relationships has a tradition of having been started by some non-human creature, usually as an animal that married a woman....The ruling family, for example, is thought to be descended from the union of a leopard with a woman....[3]

The Dahomeans are representative of variant characteristics of the thousands of basic forms of the religions indigenous to Africa. Further study will demonstrate that African religion is part of the total mosaic of life, not a mere thread in the fabric.

Conclusion....

The African bushman who consults his shaman is doing what his forefathers have done for millenia. There is nothing "primitive" or "savage" about that practice. Perhaps when European and American

---

[3]Eugene A. Nida, *Understanding Animism* (New York: Friendship Press, 1959), pp. 11-20.

scholars realize this fact further, the African will be allowed to make his contribution to the sciences of healing and counseling.

BIBLIOGRAPHY

Daryll Forde, *African Worlds* (London: Oxford, 1954)
R.C. Mitchell and H.W. Turner, *Bibliography of Modern African Religious Movements* (Evanston: Northwestern University, 1967)
Benjamin C. Ray, *African Religions* (Englewood Cliffs: Prentice Hall, 1976)
Robert I. Rotberg (editor) *Rebellion in Black Africa* (London: Oxford, 1975)

Ajak:
My name is Ajak and I am a twenty-year-old part of the Dinka peoples. A year ago I went into a major city to seek work. In that lonely place I got worried about my family back in our village. Even though I wanted to earn more money than anyone ever has in my family, I got little news from home.

I was so much in turmoil that a city shaman from our clan diagnosed me as being possessed with an evil spirit. I was, I admit, running around in circles outside my shack and panting heavily. That shaman began to try to cast out that evil spirit. That evil spirit continued to have dominion over me until I returned to my village and offered a sacrifice to the supreme god, Nhialic. Then the evil spirit bothered me no more.

31

John Willie:

My name is John Wille Ross, a thirty-year-old owner of a drug store in New Orleans. Mine is not an ordinary drug store. Oh, yes, I have the standard brands of decongestants, aspirin and laxatives.

However, my primary business is built on voodoo items. We have plenty of candles dedicated to saints for those who wish to mix Roman Catholicism with their animism. Mainly we sell potions of all kinds. Love, hate, accident or hexing are the favorites. We also have numerous magical powers. There are those which place the victim in a trance if thrown into his face. We also have ground frogs, lizards and rose petals for special curses or blessings. If you've never done curses or blessings, we have books of instructions.

Stop over here and you will see the latest in African dolls. One of our customers stuck a pin in one and her rival for her fiance's affections suddenly had to have her appendix removed. They work, alright, but mainly because the people around here think they do. You'll have to excuse me. I have to unload a new shipment of potions from Haiti. Do come again.

Chapter IV

Hinduism

"Hindu" comes from a Persian word meaning "Indian." Therefore, in a broad sense, Hinduism may be defined as the religion of the Indian people. This includes more than 350 million believers in India, 20 million Hindu inhabitants of Asian and African nations, not to mention some 350,000 Hindus in the Americas.

Because Hinduism is so interwoven with the Indian way of life, Hinduism can be said to be both more and less than a religion, depending on one's definition and viewpoint. Hinduism may be seen as a sociological grouping of persons quite free of any set of creeds regarding the nature and work of God. The unity of Hinduism is not built on any insistence on the existence or nonexistence of God. In this sense, the faith of the Hindus is not a religion. However, Hinduism may also be said to be more than a religion. This is true because most Hindus do hold in common certain practices, ideals, duties, beliefs and scriptures. This gives to Hinduism a basic identity even without a common view of God.

For this reason, also a definition of Hinduism is difficult to formulate. It embodies much ancient folklore of India, morés of the people, social class distinctions and even such modern reform movements as Vendanta. An attempted definition is "Hinduism is the way of life of the indigenous Indian people, incorporating numerous practices, rituals and reform movements."

Brief History....

The beginning of Hinduism is difficult to pinpoint for two reasons: it began somewhere in mythology and folklore of Indo-European peoples and has no discinct founder-prophet such as Guatama Buddha or Confucius.

The primary written source of the peoples of the Indus Valley about 2000 BC is the *Vedic* literature. Archeology and that literature tell us that these early dwellers had numerous fertility gods and goddesses.

About 1700 BC these peoples began to be invaded by waves of people they called Aryans, or "the noble ones." They came first from Persia. The Aryan invaders are pictured in the *Vedas* as nomads following their flocks.

The Aryans brought with them a caste system which they forced on the Indus Valley residents. At the top, they placed the Brahmins, highly revered priests who served the numerous Aryan deities. Also considered near the top were the chieftains and their loyal, trained warriors, call Kshatriyas. The commoners, below the priestly and warrior classes, were called Vaishyas. A fourth group was composed of the conquered peoples and were called Shudras. They were quickly made slaves of by the Aryans. This early division became the basis for the enduring caste system in India.

The Aryans, like the conquered dwellers of the Indus Valley, had a type of religion. It was mainly based on gods who were identified with such natural forces and elements as the sun, moon and soil. These gods were served through sacrifices and the drinking of a sacred liquid called soma.

The records of the Aryan-Indus mixing of religious values was recorded in the *Vedas*, which became sacred literature. They were written between 1500 and 800 BC.

The basic Vedic work is the *Rig-Veda*. It is composed of more than one thousand poems to the gods of the Aryans. Within the *Vedas* there are more than 250 poems to Indra, the conqueror of evil. One reads in part:

O Indra, in the past the
sages of old bore your Indra
power....Indra held the
earth menaced by the demons.
He fixed it and then expan-
ded it.

We prepare soma to offer
him, the author of many great
deeds, the Bull, worthy of
the soma drink. He, the hero,
takes the wealth of those
who do not perform the sacrifice to give it to those
who perform it.[1]

The Vedic period also produced the *Brahmanas*, or commentaries on sacrificial rites. In the Aryan Indus society with their roles and ideas, sacrificial ritual was emphasized as the way to God.

The later Vedic period (ca 900-700 BC) period produced the *Upanishads*. The Upanishadic period was one of emphasis on renewed inner comtemplation. A Hindu theology began to emerge. Ultimate reality was identified with *Brahman*. All other beings were described as but expressions of the impersonal god-being called *Brahman*, a neuter name meaning "ever expanding". The *Upanishads* taught that all is not *Brahman* is illusion, which is labelled maya. The masses were introduced to the idea of service as being primarily loving devotion (bhakti).

After the pre-Aryan and *Vedic* periods came the third period of Hindu history, from about 1 AD to 1800 AD. The Gupta Empire was eatablished in AD 320 and afforded Hinduism sufficient protection for development of a "golden age."

The *Sutras* (treatises on doctrinal matters) and *Puranas* (sacred legends about deities and heroes) were produced between AD 300 and 700.

Moslem invaders began to occupy parts of India during the early 8th century, AD. Particularly in northern India was territory lost to the Moslem invaders.

The Moslem leader Baber was able to consolidate northern India by 1526 AD. One of his successors, Akbar (1542-1605) granted freedom to all religions, including the new one called Sikhism.

---

[1]*Rig Veda*, 1:103.

The beginning of the nineteenth century marked the start of the fourth period in Hindu history, the modern era. Much of India came under British control during this period and India began to emerge as a nation exposed to modern Western thought. British rule began to crumble after World War I when a Hindu-Moslem rift became apparent. In the 1930's and 1940's (until 1948), a man named Mahatma Ghandi led a nonviolent civil disobedience movement while the Moslems supported the British government. By 1935, the Muslim League was insisting on an independent Muslim state to be formed in the western and eastern zones of the Indian subcontinent. In 1947, the British Indian Empire came to an end, the separate dominions of Pakistan and India came into existence. Modern India is a prime example of an emerging nation stripped of former colonialism by an outsider. Currently, modern Hinduism is a conglomeration of western idealism, ancient myths and folk mores.

Basic beliefs....

Though creeds do not compose the dominant adherent element in modern Hinduism, most Hindus today hold major areas of belief in common. The question as to whether Hinduism is monotheistic (believers in one god) is a complex one. Indian thought has consistently held since the *Upanishadic* period that god is one but has frequently experienced a deep desire to give this one god various forms and names. So, the Hindu may be said to be ''monotheistic'' if this be taken to mean that there is one basic reality (this is usually called monism), but not so if we take that term to mean that this reality can take only one form.

All Hindus hold that the nature of ultimate reality or impersonal absolute (Brahman) is unknowable by man. This same Brahman is everywhere and dwells but is not captured in everything simultaneously. Man is seen as a part of Brahman who can realize this union with God. Brahman is often described as being, bliss or awareness. Man can realize his oneness with Brahman and thereby achieve greatness through godhood.

Vishnu is worshiped as one of the gods who becomes incarnate at will and is very popular with the masses because of this power of reincarnation. Vishnu is not worshiped directly by Hindus as much as in his incarations, of which there are ten: the fish, the bear, the man-lion, the dwarf, Parasurama, Rama, Krishna, Buddha and one yet to come. (Some modern Vishunities consider Jesus of Nazareth the tenth incarnation.) The most important incarnation of Vishnu to most Vishunites, however, is Krishna. (Note: for some Krishna devotees, it is Vishnu who is an incarnation of Krishna.)

In the piece of Hindu literature most akin to the Christian scriptures, the Bhagavad-Gita, Krishna becomes the supreme god and universal savior of the human family.

Siva is another of the hundreds of gods within Hinduism. He is seen as the Creator-Destroyer-Sustainer of life. He is a popular god despite the fact that he supposedly promotes edurance of pain, self-mutilation, starvation and solitary meditation. Siva does this through his immense power and use of deception called maya.

The cosmology (view of the world's structure) of the Hindu is different from that of Jesus and his followers. Huston Smith has pointed out that the Hindus see the world as having five distinct characteristics:

1) It includes innumerable worlds horizontally, innumerable tiers

vertically and innumerable cycles temporarlly.

2) It is a moral world in which the law of Karma never wavers.

3) This is a temporary world which will never in itself replace as supreme as ultimate destination for the human spirit.

4) This world is maya, or deceptively tricky in that it passes itself off as ultimate; and,

5) This world is a training ground that can advance persons toward the Highest.[2] Therefore, the ultimate goal is not life in this world.

There is no more important belief in all of Hindu thought than that of Karma, a law which decrees that every responsible decision must have its consequences.

Karma means "action" or "doing" and is a Hindu ethical interpretation of the law of causation which reasons that every action is the effect of a cause. It is a principle of moral reaction which is applied to both good and evil actions.

One Hindu scholar says it this way, "Nothing is lost which has been earned by work; and nothing comes in which is not deserved. Every action has a double effect; it produces its appropriate reward, and it also affects character."[3]

Bound up with Karma for the Hindu is the assumption of samsara, or the rebirth or transmigration of the soul. The soul, or atman, is identical with Brahman, but distinct from the self which transmigrates from body to body, carrying with it its load of karma from previous lives.

According to karma, a person may be reborn as a god, up or down in the caste system, or even as an animal, according to his every past thought, word and deed. In the future, the tendencies of this present life will work themselves out in the next one.

Karma also in the present determines the acts appropriate to each caste. What is right for the Brahman may be wrong for the commoner.

What persons desire most is deliverance or Moksha, from the endless cycle or reincarnation governed by Karma and the limitations of individual existence.

Another common belief held by most modern Hindus is their view of persons. This begins with the atman, or "Inner self." Each person is held by Hindus to be a layered being composed of a physical body, consicious personality and a subconscious personality. So, in order to be his "real" self, one is to realize his innate godness by not confusing his real self (atman) with his outward self.

Realization of self and escape from reincarnation can come in one of four ways to the Hindu: through works (Karma Yoga) such as showing hospitality to one's neighbor; through knowledge (Jnana Yoga) by deep meditation; through devotion (Bhakti Yoga) by loving God for no ulterior reason or through psychologically righting oneself (Raga Yoga). Note that all these efforts come under the broad heading of Yoga, (meaning "union through discipline"). This is the term used for working out one's escape from this limited life. So, this life is not what each person is searching for, but he desires, instead, escape from this life to a higher level of godlike existence.

---

[2]Huston, Smith, *The Religions of Man* (New York: Harper and Row Publisher, 1958), P. 85.

[3]T.M.P. Mahadevan, *Outlines of Hinduism* (Bombay: Chetana, 1860) P. 59.

So, the message of Hinduism seems to be something like this: live out life doing what is known to be right so that finally entry may be made into eternal peace through deliverance from the limitations of this present deceptive life.

Reform movements....

At least three major world religions began as reform movements within Hinduism. Guatama Buddha began the movement named for him as a protest against the rigid worship patterns and caste distinctions of his day. In the same century (6th BC), one Mahavira preached that salvation is to be won through self-denial. The movement called Jainism emerged from his example and teachings. The newest major world religion, Sikhism, was founded by Nanak, a contemporary of Martin Luther in the early sixteenth century. Sikhism was started as a reform movement within Hinduism, initially as an attempt to combine Islam and Hinduism. (A chapter is given later in this book to each of these three important reform movements within Hinduism).

Hinduism has also experienced modern reform movements such as Brahmo Samaj. Started in 1828 by Ram Mohan Roy. He was born in 1772 in west Bengal. By the time he was eighteen years old, he had mastered several languages, including Arabic and English.

In 1820, Ram Mohan Roy published *The Precepts of Jesus, the Guide to Peace and Happiness*. It consisted of a compilation of verses from the New Testament with their Sanskirt and Bengali translations. Later in 1820, he wrote that he believed in the message of Jesus and the truths revealed in the Christian system. However, he also wrote that he could not subscribe to the idea of three gods in one godhead. Since he could not endorse the Christian concept of the Trinity, he played a major role in establishing a Unitarian Committee in Calcutta for advancing the cause of education.

Ram Mohan Roy was a student of Islam, Christianity, Judasim and Hinduism. His religious ideas compiled from all four of these were merged into the Brahmo Samaj, or "Society of God," which he started in 1828. He preached that the basis of all religion is love and charity. Most experts on Hinduism feel that Rom Mohan Roy stands as a bridge between the past and future of Hinduism. For this reason, Rom Mohan Roy was a significant reformer within Hinduism.

Another modern reform movement for Hinduism is the Arya Samaj. It has combined social reform and a renewed pride in being Hindu. The founder of Arya Samaj. Sarasvati, called for a return to ancient Hindu literature. When the movement was started in 1875, its slogan was "Back to the Vedas." Sarasvati campaigned for a monotheistic form of Hindu universalism open to all, regardles of caste or nationality. Later, the Arya Samaj became an intolerant and aggressively anti-foreign movement. In a special ceremony it invests the "untouchables" with a sacred thread, making them equal to Hindus within the caste system. Arya Samaj also has the goal of reconverting Moslems and Christians to the Hindu faith. In north India, the movement has successfully restricted the growth of the Christian churches.

An outstanding reformer of Hinduism was Mahatma Ghandi, who stressed nonviolence as a form of social protest. This man who became a symbol of reaction against injustice was refused service on a train in South Africa in 1893. He led a movement which struck the coal mines, sugar plantations and railroads.

Ghandi soon returned to India and began to teach that the "untouchables", members of the lowest caste, were *Harijan*, or God's people." This led to the beginning of a major social revolution in India. Ghandi refused to accept Christianity as a religious system, but readily and thoroughly accepted the teachings of Jesus.

Often overlooked in America is Rabindranath Tagore (1861-1941). Tagore was a poet, novelist, dramatist, actor, composer, educator, philosopher, painter, prophet, mystic and a great lover of nature and beauty. Tagore interpreted the *Upanishads* for the modern world in the light of his experiences. He sought to demonstrate his religious philosophy by establishing a school in Bengal in which the pupils, through contact with nature, were led to experience the divine. He taught that salvation is both for the individual and the community.

Conclusion....

Hinduism is one of the world's oldest religions and appears to be growing, especially in the western world. It is as diverse as the Bengali businessman who begins each day with an hour long traditional puja (or ritual based on a godshelf) to the villager whose Karma is a mixture of rural folkways and the classic Hinduism of the *Vedas.*

The Hindu has asked and found answers to some of the most profound questions in life. Great teachers have led him to such high moments as when Ghandi said, "God can never be realized by one who is not pure in heart. Self-purification therefore must mean purification in all the walks of life." [4]

BIBLIOGRAPHY

Swami Nikhilananda, *Hinduism; Its Meaning for the Liberation of the Spirit* (New York: Harper and Brother, 1958)
Swami Radhakrishnan, *The Hindu View of Life* (New York: The Macmaillan Co., 1927)
D.S. Sarma, *Hinduism Through the Ages.* (Thompson, Conn., Inter-Culture Press, 1973)
K.M. Sen, *Hinduism* (Baltimore: Penguin Books, 1962)

---

[4]Louis Renou, (editor) *Hinduism* (New York: George Braziller, 1962).

Raji:

My name is Raji. I am a ten-year-old "street rat" in Calcutta. It is my responsibility to care for and feed my two younger brothers and a sister. I steal, beg and lie to feed myself and them. Every day I see dead bodies on the street. My elders tell me that I must have done something horrible in a previous life to be born in Calcutta.

The university professors across town see themselves as Brahmin and they speak of Moksha and maya. The world is evil alright. I hope it is not too cold tonight as we have to find another place to sleep on the streets.

In my next life, I hope to do better. If I can just stay true to karma, it will happen. They say I'm smart for a ten-year-old with no schooling, so maybe next time I can be a Brahmin. That would really be something. But, for now....

Bal:

My name is Bal. I am a guru. My devotees call me the "Perfect Master." In return I demand that they surrender their minds and bodies to me without reservation. As their guru, I help them see the same "divine light" which I have seen and to hear the secret sound or the unique "Holy Name." On occasion, I can also help people open their "third eye" and obtain secret knowledge through certain secret ceremonies in which they have secret estatic experiences which I cannot describe here, since they are secret.

Sometimes thousands gather around my ashram, or retreat center. Perhaps you would join those. It could lead to an escape from karma and samsara through moksha.

Chapter V

Jainism

There were two vital and lasting reform movements within Hinduism in the sixth century, BC. Both of them denied the validity of the *Vedas* as religious literature and both rejected the traditional caste system. One is today called Buddhism. The other is Jainism.

A common misunderstanding often perpetuated in the study of world religions is that one Mahavira was its founder. Actually, the person Mahavira was an important reformer in a whole series of Jinas.

The man Mahavira was given the title "Tirthankara," but there were twenty-four of them for every era. Today Jains claim that their religion is eternal. The first person with that title was Rsabha, who is said in Jain legend to have lived for 8,400,000 years. In succession, twenty-three others have lived. Each one lives for a shorter period of time. Mahavira, the twenty-fouth and last for this era, lived but seventy-two years.

Modern Jain historians confirm the historicity of only the last two Tirtankaras; i.e., of one Parsua and one Mahavira, although the popular Jain would probably contend for the actual existence of all twenty-four.

Mahavira was an older contemporary of Guatama, the Buddha. His dates, according to Jain tradition, 599-527 BC.

The Jain movement currently numbers about 1.5 million in India. Today Jains are known as successful merchants and wealthy bankers. This is ironic, because the movement started as an ascetic one, denying any value to money and possessions.

At about age thirty, Mahavira became a monk and instituted an order for laymen and monks. The order included men and women. He was so successful that by his death he had enrolled fourteen thousand monks.

Mahavira was born with the given name of Vardhamana, but was given the title Mahavira, meaning "great hero."

Mahavira was known as a Tirthankara, or "one who shows the true way through the ocean of life." Persons with the same title play an important part in Jain life today.

Mahavira taught his monks that they themselves were divine. There task was to let the essential deity within them come to its own. Mahavira frequently said, "There is no higher god than man himself." Religion, for Mahavira, is self-development with little or no dependence on outsider or higher powers. In Mahavira's words, "The pure, all-conscious, self-absorbed soul is god and never less or more."

Legend surrounds the life of Mahavira. It is said that his parents were such strict ascetics that they eventually fasted to death.

Mahavira, it is said, went about nude and swept the paths before him so as not to step on insects, strained his food with a cloth and wore a cloth over his month so as not to draw insects into his mouth. Under a tree near a river bank, he finally gained enlightenment. There he became a Jina, or "conqueror of evil." At the place of his death, it is said that the marks in the stone there are Mahavira's footprints. He died of self-starvation at the age of seventy-two in the small town of Pava.

The Jains gained strength during the Mauryan dynasty (322-183 BC). It was during this era that the Jain community was divided into the two major sects that prevail today. The occasion of the division was the exodus of many Jain monks from the Ganges to the Deccan, where the Jain faith spread. The emigrants retained the rule nudity established by Mahavira. Those who remained in the north disregarded this rule and allowed their monks to wear clothes. They were called "white clad." The nude monks of the south were known as "sky-clad."

Basic beliefs....

The modern Jain system of thought turns on seven concepts:
1) *Jiva*

This word may be defined as "life, vitality, soul or consciousness." Jains reject the Hindu gods, including the highest one, Brahman. Instead, Jains stress Jiva, with its accompanying idea of the eternity of the soul, or Atman. Jains maintain that there are numerous Jivas, all independent and eternal. All animal life is seen as having Jiva. Therefore, no animal is to be molested. Even certain vegetables are included and great care must be taken no to injure them.

2) *Ajiva*

The word means, "things inanimate." Jainism has an elaborate classification of natural objects, or those without a Jiva, or soul. One such category of inanimate objects is Pudgaca, or "matter which possesses color, taste, smell and form." Defining Jiva and Ajiva as they do, Jains have a dualistic version of life. Jiva is life, eternal and positive. Ajiva is lifeless, therefore, material and evil. The entire universe is divided between life and not-life.

3) *Punya*

The word means "merit" and is used by Jains to mean the actions which lend to good karma, out of which comes peace of mind. Among these meritorious acts are giving water to the thirsty and thinking well of everyone.

4) *Papa*

The word translates as "sin" and it is here that the chief characteristic of Jainism comes to light, that of reverence for life. The most hideous sin is the taking of any life. However, Jain teachings list seventeen other grevious sins. Included on the list are: untruthfulness, excessive love of possessions, anger, greed, cheating, slander, lack of self-control, hypocrisy and lack of integrity in faith.

5) *Asrava*

This word is used to describe the way karma is acquired by the soul. This is a negative term, since karma is viewed as evil.

6) *Karma*

The Jain defines karma differently than does the Hindu. (To use the same term with a different meaning is a technique employed frequently by reformers.) For Mahavira and the Jains, karma consists of extremely subtle matter which infiltrates into the soul whenever worldly actions make an opening for it. The Jain sees himself as surrounded by karma and must be constantly on guard, lest karma penetrate his being through Asrava. Jains believe that there are eight distinct kinds of karma, each of which is harmful in its own unique manner.

7) *Moksha*

Moksha means "release." When a strict Jain ascetic has attained Moksha, he at once becomes a Siddha. This is a being without caste, unaffected by smell. He is without the sense of taste, feeling, hunger, form, pain, sorrow, joy, birth or old age. He is described as enjoying an endless calm and is without body and the presence of karma.

In summary, the Jain sees all persons as souls encased in evil matter. Thus, the goal of Jainism is to liberate the soul from matter. Mahavira set the model by turning his back on the wealth of his home and submitting his body to rigorous discipline.

Jains have no need for a Creator since they are matter as eternal. Each one works out his own salvation through asceticism.

Jain Monks....

The monk remains the ideal for the Jain community today. He takes five vows:

1) *Ahimsa*

Over the entrance to many Jain temples is the text, "Non-injury is the ultimate good of all life." This concept of Ahimsa, or "non-injury" is the chief contribution of Jainism to all other world religions. A Jain monk will take drastic measures to avoid harming any living being. They are vegetarian and avoid the use of leather since a life must be taken before it can be made. The strictest Jain monks still sweep the path before them with a straw carefully before they take the next step, so as to avoid destruction or suffering for any insect life. In some Jain temples rats are fed. Mahatma Ghandi, Albert Schweitzer and Martin Luther King, Jr., were all twentieth century heirs to the Jain concept of non-injury.

2) *Truth*

Jain monks must speak the truth, period!

3) *Theft*

Jain monks are world-renouned for their refusal to take anything that has not been given the them.

4) *Sex*

Jain monks renounce sexual pleasures. Some of the more conservative Jain orders will not allow any woman to seek salvation in a monastery. This is ironic, since Mahavira even recruited women for his first order of monks.

5) *Renouncing all attachments...*

It is said that Mahavira renounced all attachments and even refused to stay in one place for more than one day at a time lest he build false, enduring attachments to any person or thing. The modern Jain monk believes that attachments to other persons and objects is one of the dangerous elements that allows karma to seep into his soul.

Jain Literature....

A sampling of Jain literature is helpful in getting a "feel" for Jain beliefs. The Jain canon consists of forty-five texts of a few pages each.

One of these texts is the "Book of Sermons." It contains this section:

> He who grasps at even a
> little, whether living or
> lifeless, or consents to
> another doing so, will never
> be freed from sorrow.

and

> Even plants are beings,
> capable of growth.
> Their bodies need food.
> They are individuals.
> The reckless cut them for
>   their own pleasure
> And slay many living things
>   in doing so.

From the "Book of Good Conduct" comes the saying, "Injury to the earth is like striking, cutting, maiming or killing a blind man."

From the "Book of Laten Instructions" can be read:

When a monk has left his children wives, and has given up wordly actions, nothing is pleasant to him, nothing unpleasant...

Though a man conquer a thousand brave foes in battle,
If he conquers only himself, this is his greatest conquest.
Battle with yourself! Or what use is fighting others?
He who conquers himself by himself will win happiness...

From the "Nectar of Aphorisms of Polity" the Jain learns what the good ruler is to be like:

The king who thinks only of filling his belly is abandoned even by his queen.

A king's order is a wall which none can climb. He should not tolerate even a son who disobeys his commands.

He should never be improper in dress or manners.

When the king is deceitfull, who will not be deceitful?

From the "Lawbook of Manu," there are Jain sayings on war:

The force of arms cannot do what peace does. If you can gain your desired end with sugar, why use poison?

In union is strength. Even a mad elephant will trip on a twisted clump of grass.

Conclusion....

Today Jainism is but a minority sect in Hinduism. The majority of the Jains live in or near Bombay in modern India. The Jains are known as excellent businessmen. This is ironic since Mahavira taught that material blessings are to be avoided.

Changing by the times into wealthy merchants, the Jains see "non-injury" as central to their religion. All of life is to be respected. In the midst of this respect. the Jain seeks Moksha through the avoidance of the evil force of *karma*.

BIBLIOGRAPHY

A.L. Basham, *The Wonder That Was India* (New York: Grove Press, Inc., 1959)

A. Chakravarti, *A Religion of Ahimsa* (Bombay: Rantanchand Hirachand, 1957)

Louis Renou, *Religions of Ancient India* (London: Oxford, 1953)

H. Zamier, *Philosophies of India* (New York: Meridian Books, 1957)

Mahavra:

My name is Mahavra. I am a thirty-year-old Jain merchant in Bombay. When I was younger as a university student in Bombay, I considered several careers. For awhile I considered becoming a Jain monk, but I found the demands to be too strict. The occupations of tanner and butcher I found lucrative but running opposed to our Jain concept of non-injury to all life.

My business is good, even among the Hindu clientele, because we Jains have a deserved reputation for honesty in business.

Frequently westerners ask me about salvation. I guess you could say I am on my own without much help from monks or sacred literature. My primary problem is that it is constantly a temptation to allow karma to permeate my being by becoming attached to all that is around me, particularly my business.

Mahavira:

I am a sixty-five-year-old member of the Digambara sect of Jainism. I live in a remote part of southern India and am one of the fewer than three hundred nude or ''sky-clad'' monks of modern Jainism. My nudity is a sign of great holiness and respect from the other monks in our order.

There are no women in our order since they are the greatest of all temptations in this karma-filled world. It is our belief that our model, Mahavira, was never married, in spite of rumors to the contrary. We do not even allow women to enter into our Jain temples.

Westerners seem obsessed with the idea of my nudity. It is a natural result of our beliefs about self-denial. We have an intense respect for all life. Nudity is a sign of my combination of self-denial and respect for all other life. This aids me in my respect for Moksha.

Chapter VI

Sikhism

Sikhism is one of the latest (with the single exception of the Bahai World Faith) of all of the major world religions. It had its start in the Punjab in north India in the fifteenth century, AD. Moslems had come to this area with even more intensity beginning with the tenth century, AD. Moslem mystics, called Sufis, had begun to converse with Hindu gurus. It was almost inevitable that some synthesis begin to occur between the two strong traditions.

One who was interested in such a synthesis was Kabir, of the early fifteenth century. Kabir was a Moslem from Benares who became a disciple of the Hindu teacher Ramananda. He soon concluded that there is truth in all religions and that there is but one God known variously as Allah, Rama or Krishna. Kabir remained a monotheist, believing in the one true God. Many of his poems were incorporated into the Sikh scriptures.

Nanak (1469-1538) was a younger contemporary of Kabir. He was born a Hindu but influenced by Islam. He was married, with two children, when he left home to serch for religious truth. He wandered about wearing the prayer beads of the Moslem and the saffron-robe of the Hindu. He visited Benares as a Hindu holy place and made a pilgrimage to Mecca. At the Kaaba stone in Mecca, he lay down with his feet toward it. Being rebuked and kicked in the side by a devout Moslem, Nanak said, ''Turn me in the direction in which God is not.''

Nanak's conversion experience came when he went to bathe in a river. There he saw God holding up to him a cup of nector and saying, ''Go and repeat my name and make others do so.'' Nanak then toured northern India, declaring that there is no Moslem or Hindu, but all follow after the one true God. He was at first persecuted by both Moslems and Hindus. He had little success outside his own native territory of Punjab. This was in spite of the fact that his sermonic style was that of the Hindu poet accompanied by a Moslem drummer boy.

When Nanak died in 1538, both Hindus and Moslems claimed the body. It was decided that the argument would be settled by having both groups bring fresh flowers to the grave. Whichever group of flowers lasted longest, that group could claim the body. It is said that both groups of cut flowers stayed fresh for more than a year. Nanak was neither a Moslem nor a Hindu even in death.

Nanak is always called ''guru'' and his followers are Sikhs (disciples. The first nine successors of Nanak are also called ''guru'' and Sikhs believe that his powers and presence resided in them.

Under the British Empire the Sikhs were favored as good soldiers and skilled mechanics. However, at the partition of India and Pakistan in 1947, the Sikhs rose in arms to claim a state of their own. The Sikhs were defeated. Tens of thousands of them had to flee across dusty plains to Amritsar. Today the Indian Sikhs live mainly in that area without any inclination of the Indian government to grant them a separate state.

Basic beliefs....

The primary source of Sikh teaching is the holy book called the *Adi Granth*, a collection of Kabir's and Nanak's sayings plus those of numerous other Sikh, Jain and Hindu sages.

The fundamental teaching in the *Adi Granth* is "God the True Name." This was an attempt to say that God is greater than any of the names by which he has become known to man, such as Allah and Krishna. Nanak's poems are full of Moslem monotheistic assumptions, such as calling God Creator and Lord. These are combined with the Hindu assumption that God is the formless one pervading all things.

When speaking of the world, Nanak spoke alternately of both Hindu *maya* and Moslem creation. This is seen clearly in his saying:

Maya, the mythical goddess,
Sprang from the One,
and her womb brought forth
Three acceptable disciples of
the One:
Brahma, Visnu and Shiva.[1]

A prominent teaching of Nanak which was taken from both Moslem and Hindu sources was that of the need for a guru to sistain personal relationships with his disciples. In this tradition, the Sikh guru has been a charismatic leader of the people in both war and peace.

Further, Sikhism has given its own unique definition to the word "guru." The word is defined more in terms of influence than office. That influence is necessary to lead persons to God. Nanak taught:

O Man, repeat God's name and
praises;
But how shall you obtain this
pleasure without the guru?
It is the guru who unites man
with God.[2]

Nanak never tired of condemning empty ritual in religion. For him, rejection of ritual would bring about a revival in true religion, i.e., doing deeds of kindness and mercy. In this vein, Nanak remained within the world and counseled his followers to do the same. He openly rejected asceticism, calling instead for a vital faith concerned with bringing love and justice to the world.

---

[1]Trilochan Singh, *Selections from the Sacred Writings of the Sikhs* (London: George Allen and Unwin, Ltd. 1960) p. 46.

[2]William T. deBary (editor) *Sources of Indian Tradition.* (New York: Columbia University Press, 1958) p. 532.

One of Nanak's most expressive poems captures the spirit of his theology:

> To sing truly of the tran-
>   scendent Lord,
> Would exhaust all vocabu-
>   laries,
> All human powers of expression,
> Myriads have sung of Him in
>   innumerable strains.
> His gifts to us flow in such
>   plenitude
> That man wearies of receiving
>   what God bestows;
> Age on unending age,
> Man lives on is His bounty. [3]

Sikh Worship....

The most famous shrine of the Sikhs is the Golden Temple in Amristar in north India. It is a small building set in the middle of a man-made lake. One comes first to a gateway guarded by an armed Sikh. He then follows a causeway leading to the temple proper. The walls and domes of the upper half of the temple are covered with gold. The temple, unlike Hindu ones, contains no images. Instead, the focal point of worship is the *Adi Granth*, the sacred book, which is chanted constantly by readers.

Sikhs come to the temple and show their reverence for the scripture by bowing with folded hands in the common Indian salutation. Prayers may be said both at the Golden Temple and at home.

Daily rituals for Sikhs include a morning bath followed by the reading of prayers. When Sikhs gather for communal worship, they meet in local temples called gurudwaras. There is usually prayers, reading of the *Adi Granth*, a sermon and a communal meal. There are no Sikh priests and worship is kept simple so as to be led with ease by untrained laymen.

Sikhism Today....

Nanak was succeeded in order by nine men called "gurus." The tenth was Gobind Singh (1666-1708). Gobind Singh or "Gobind the Lion" was a talented writer or verse and a courageous leader in the military sense. In 1699, Singh started the Khalsa, or "Comminity of the Pure." Initiation was by a new ritual called the "Baptism of the Sword." Five symbols were part of the Khalsa from the beginning. They are:

1) Kes - unshorn hair and beard
2) Kangha - to keep the hair tidy
3) Kach - knee-length breeches (from which the English word "Khaki" comes)
4) Kara - a steel bracelet worn on the right wrist; and,
5) Kirpan - the sword.

---

[3]Trilochan Singh and others, *Adi Granth* (New York: The Macmillan Co., 1960) p. 30.

The members of the Khalsa were also to observe four rules:
1) Refraining from cutting any hair of the body
2) Refraining from smoking or chewing tobacco or the drinking of alcohol.
3) Refraining from the eating of any meat slaughtered by the customary Mulsim bleeding to death.
4) Refraining from molesting any Moslem women or have sexual relations with any woman other than one's lawful wife.

Thus was begun the new Sikh order of fighting men. Membership in the group was kept open and there was soon gathered hundreds of fearless fighting men. Gobind Singh was assassinated by a Moslem fanatic in 1708.

As a mixture of Nanak's peaceful syncretism and Gobind Singh's militant brotherhood, about six million Sikhs live in today's world. They are chiefly seen as a visible minority in a Hindu world.

Most of the Sikh males are farmers, mechanics and soldiers. These persons are found chiefly in three religious sects. They are the Udasis, the Sahajdharis and the Singhs. The Udasis are basically an order of holy men. They are known by the wearing of coarse, yellow garments. Unlike most other Sikhs, they do shave their heads and beards. The Sahajdharis, or "slow goers," reject the militancy of the Singhs and are usually clean shaven. The Singhs take pride in their rich heritage of group identity.

Conclusion....
Sikhism has seen itself go from a passive sect to a militant order in a matter of four centuries. Nanak's teachings on syncretism are mixed with simple daily ritual and a determination to survive. These are the Sikhs of today.

BIBLIOGRAPHY

J.C. Archer, *The Sikhs* (Princeton: University Press, 1946)
H.R. Gupta, *History of the Sikhs* (New York: Dawson, 1950)
Harbans Singh, *The Heritage of the Sikhs* (Bombay: 1964)
Khushmant Singh, *The Sikhs* (London: George Allen and Unwin, 1953)
Khushmant Singh, *The Sikhs Today* (Calcutta: Orient Longmans, 1964)

Bahadur Singh:

My name is Bahadur Singh. I am a thirty-four-year-old resident of Kenya where I am the best mechanic in the city. I am glad to be a Sikh. I gives one pleasure to know that he is part of a great religious heritage such as the Sikhs.

I am a part of the Singh sect within Sikhism. I am known on the street and easily discernible from the Hindus and Moslems here by my magnificient beard. The bracelet on my right wrist and head of uncut hair also speak of my religious preference.

We Sikhs expect one day to have a homeland in the north of India and we will fight to get it if we have to. We have fought in the past to survive and I would gladly leave Kenya to fight again if necessary. Please excuse me. It is time for my evening prayers and reading of the *Adi Granth*.

Tegh Kishan:

My name is Tegh Kishan and I am an eighteen-year-old farmer's son in the Punjab of northern India. We are glad to be Sikhs of the Sahajdhari order. Others call us the "slow going ones." It is primarily the Singhs who label us such because we refuse to be a part of their military emphases. There is no doubt that we are nearer to the teachings of the peaceful Nanak.

It is our purpose to walk the way between the Moslems and the Hindus, the way to the true God. We would like to live in peace with all persons, something we have not been able to do often in the past.

Next year I will make a pilgrimage to our Golden Temple. It will be something I will remember the rest of my life. In the meantime, I will learn to be the best farmer in our region.

Chapter VII

Vedanta

For almost a century, militant Hinduism has been present in the United States in the form of a message called Vedanta and the agent is the Ramakrishna Mission. It was founded and got its name from Ramakrishna (1836-1886), a remarkable guru. In spite of almost no education, Ramakrishna became enlightened through worship of the mysterious goddess, Kali. He revered her as the divine mother of the universe. Ramakrishna tried the way of other Hindu cults with variant types of yoga. He also tasted of Islam and Christianity and announced that he had found union with the Moslem Allah and the Christians' God. The result of this search was Ramakrishna's announcement that the harmony of all religions was a fact. He said, "Different creeds are but different paths to reach the one God."

Ramakrishna gathered dozens of disciples about him. The most outstanding one was Swami Vivekananda (1863-1900). It was he who was commissioned to spread Vedanta through a missionary invasion of the western world, especially the United States.

Vivekananda introduced Vedanta to the United States at the World Parliament of Religions in 1893 held in conjunction with the World's Fair in Chicago in 1893. In the next three years, Vivekananda continued to captivate audiences and make converts to Vedanta. In 1896, he founded the Vedanta Society of New York.

In 1978, the Ramakrishna mission has more than 150 centers, with more than sixty of them outside India. These centers form the focal points for the Vedanta activities of transplanting Indian culture and religion, schools, medical treatment and social welfare. In the United States, the work has been primarily that of publishing and distributing literature.

Vedanta tenets....

There are a dozen major tenets of Vedantist philosophy which are easily discernible, even if Vedantists frequently argue that theirs is a noncreedal form of religious experience. These dozen are:

1) Ultimate Reality, that which alone has real existence is pure Spirit, pure Being. It is frequently said by Vedantists that God is an infinite circle whose center is everywhere and whose circumference is nowhere. It follows that the God which persons currently know is not pure Being, that is, is not truly God. Persons only know a fraction of his being. Further, it is held that God is not a person, but is endowed with such human attributes as love and mercy. This one God has

assumed many forms for the welfare of his devotees. They may be known as Jehovah, Allah, Siva, Kali and Visnu and are as real as any entity in the universe. It should also be noted that, for Vedantists, there are other manifestations of God currently unknown to ordinary human minds.

2) The physical universe is an appearance which disappears when full knowledge of the real is attained. A classic Hindu document, the Katha Upanishad, is frequently quoted, "Rare is the wise man who, desiring immortality, shuts his eyes to outward things and so beholds the glory of the Atman within." It is reasoned by Vedantist teachers that God is realized only by shutting our minds to outward things and turning within to abiding reality.

3) Ultimate Reality, the Supreme Being, is the creator, preserver and absorber of the universe and is manifest in the physical world as the one all-pervasive Self.

4) Persons are essentially divine. This makes the inner self of persons as identical with the one world Self. Vivekavanda said, "Man is like a infinite spring, coiled up in a small box, and that spring is trying to unfold itself." For Vedanta, when this struggle becomes a conscious effort, it is religious. A basic purpose of Vedanta is to make this effort toward God-realization a conscious one.

5) To realize one's essential deity is the supreme end of human life. For the Vedantist, this relization is done partially through the overcoming of ignorance. It is held that, in most human lives, ignorance covers one's true nature as God. Ignorance is sometimes pictured as a strong drink, making one forget and instead create strong fantasies about "reality." Man's basic problem is that through ignorance he had identified his true self with his body, his senses, his mind or worst of all, his ego. This ignorance and its results must be overcome to realize one's innate deity.

6) The methods of this desired God-relization vary according to the different tendencies and capacities of those aspiring to it. Each may grow at his own rate of speed and in his own direction, as long as the ultimate goal of knowing oneself as God is moved toward.

7) All the different religions are but different ways leading ultimately to God. Condemned is the arrogant spirit of sectarianism. It is argued that religion is like poetry, it is an individual expression. It is argued, further, that when a religion develops the ambition of imposing its doctrine on all mankind, it degrades itself into a tyrany and becomes a form of imperialism.

The mystic poet of medieval India, Kabir, wrote:

The jewel is lost in the
mud, and all are seeking for
it; some look for it in the
east, and some in the west;
some in the water and some
amongst stones.[1]

---

[1]Quoted by Rabindra Nath Tagore in an address given at the Sri Ramakrishna Centenary Parliament of Religions, 1936.

8) Efforts to convert members of one religion to another are expressions of intollerance and bigotry. Christianity is particularly singled out for attack as showing bigotry by attempting to convert. Christopher Underwood, in his Introduction to a collection of essays entitled *Vedanta for Modern Man*, says, "As far as organized Christianity is concerned, Vedanta would seem to have very little chance of a hearing. The cult of Christ, as preached by the Catholic and Protestant churches, is an exclusive cult. It cannot accept the Vedantist's acceptance of other Divine Incarnations...." [2]

9) Reincarnation. Vedantists argue that the cycle of births and deaths, involving experiences both pleasurable and painful, is a necessary evil. It prepares the soul on its onward march purifying and disciplining it. The goal is for the soul to become whole again by reaching its ultimate destiny, Godhood.

10) Japam. Chanting the names of God is practiced by a significant number of Vedantists. Swami Ramakrishna taught, "while practicing japam try to keep the mind fixed in the shining form of the chosen ideal.... The lord sees the heart of the devotee, not the number of times he repeats His name or how long he sits in one position." [3] Chanting the names of God is an approved method of realizing one's innate Godhood.

11) Monism. For the Vedantist, all Reality is One. It is nondualistic. Brahman (God) is ultimate reality who exists with no second. The Vedanta devotee makes this statement, "Brahman is existence."

12) Religion. For the Vedantist, religion is not submission to authority or a creed. The true religionist is who is involved in the deepening of self-awareness and the realization of one's full potential. Religion of the Vedantists involves the redemption of the entire being.

Many have noted parallels between Vedanta and Zen (see chapter on Zen in this book). One of those areas of agreement is regarding the gaining of religious knowledge. The Vedantist would likely quote the *Kana Upanishad*:

He who thinks that Brahman
is not comprehended, by him
Brahman is comprehended; but
he who thinks that Brahman
is comprehended knows It not.
Brahman is unknown to those
who know It, and known to
those who do not know It at
all.

This is parallel to an old Zen saying, "If you want to see into it, see into it directly. When you begin to think about it, it is altogether missed."

The Vedanta system of thought may be summarized: All persons are innately divine. The basic purpose of religion is the conscious

---

[2]Introduction, "Vedanta for Modern Man", Christopher Underwood, (editor) (New York: Mentor Books, 1951), pp. 12-13.

[3]"Memories of Swami Shivananda" Underwood, *Ibid*, p. 190.

realization of this deity within. Such realization comes to persons in various ways in various lives. This is evidence that the many world religions are but different paths to the same goal.

Vedanta's influence....

Vedanta has had a strong influence on twentieth century religion, especially in America. With its motto, "Up, India and conquer the world!", Vedanta grows because of its agressive distribution of literature. Vedanta has led to a common idea in today's United States that all religions are but different roads to God. This is demonstrated by the observation of D.T. Niles, a veteran Christian Indian missionary to Ceylon who visited America. He said, "I have never seen a purer version of Vedanta than the popular version of religion in America."[4]

BIBLIOGRAPHY

Swami Nikhilananda, *Hinduism: Its Meaning for the Liberation of the Spirit* (New York: Harper and Brothers, 1958)

Swami Radharkishnan, *The Hindu View of Life* (New York: The Macmillan Co., 1927)

Swami Radhakrishnan, *An Idealist View of Life* (London: George Allen and Armin, 1929)

Christopher Underwood, *Vedanta for Modern Man* (New York: Mentor Books, 1951)

Terry:

My name is Terry. I am a nineteen-year-old resident of Los Angeles. I don't know about all this Vedanta talk. I've tried a little Krishna and a little Zen. They are all OK. After all, we're all in this world together. It's different strokes for different folks, you know. We are all hunting for God in our own way. You do your thing and I'll do mine. It doesn't make that much difference. The main thing is being happy.

Let me tell you about religion. The way I see it, we're all part of God. All this talk I used to hear about sin, that's so much junk. The main thing you got to do is work things out for yourself. No one can really help you. Vedanta? I may look into that someday. Right now I'm learning to chant my mantra. After all, it makes no difference how you chant.

Ramakrishnan:

My name is Ramakrishnan and I live in New York City. I am twenty-three years old and work in the mailout center for Vedanta literature. I first got interested in Vedanta in college when I attended a lecture. The speaker told all of us we are god but we just don't know it. At that time I was into material things. I immediately sold my Corvette and gave away a lot of my clothes. Then I came to New York where I studied Vedanta for six months. The literature helped but the positive spirit of the workers around here was of the greatest benefit.

I guess I'll stay here for a while until more of my self is realized. I am just now learning Japam. Excuse me, I have to practice it now.

---

[4]Quoted in Edmund Perry, *The Gospel in Dispute* (Garden City: Doubleday and Co., 1958), p. 15.

Chapter VIII

Buddhism

Today Buddhism is definitely a *world* religion from at least two perspectives: Buddhists maintain that their teachings may be applied to any culture or person *and* Buddhism includes among its followers persons from many nations.

The more than three hundred million Buddhists in today's world form a vast chain linking countless sects and emphases, but all pointing back to the original Buddha - one Siddhartha Gautama.

Brief history....

Although there are few Buddhists in modern India, Buddhism is the offspring of Hinduism and of India.

The word "Buddha" is not a name but a title. It means the "Enlightened One" and is used to designate one Siddharta Gautama, born about 563 BC on the borders of Nepal. His family belonged to the Sakya clan or tribe, so that he is sometimes called, "Sakyamuni," the sage of the Sakyas.

Numerous legends have built up about the life of Buddha, especially concerning his youth and active ministry, but there are common details in most of the myths. It appears that his early life was spent in ease and luxury because his father was determined that Gautama should be exposed to both ease and luxury and never to such negative aspects as pain and death. Legend has it that at Buddha's birth his father was visited by an angel who offered him the choice of training his son to be a major political reformer or religious leader. Gautama's father chose the political career for his son and tried to do all in his power to keep the boy from becoming a monk.

In his teen years, Guatama married his cousin, Yasodhara and they moved into a beautiful palace built by his father. The couple enjoyed the gracious life of the elite and soon a son was born whom they named Rahula, "the Fetter."

Of all the calls in world religion history, perhaps the one of Gautama and "The Four Passing Sights" is the most beautiful. One day, in spite of his father's attempts to shield him from sighting of pain, old age and death, the young man saw an old man, a sick man, a dead man and a begging monk - in rapid succession. For the first time in his life, Guatama was forced with the negative realities of existence.

A few days later, still shaken by the four sights, he left home to search for religious meaning. At this time he was twenty-nine. "Buddha" tried intensive study under the tutelage of two famous

Brahmin monks, but was unsatisfied because they were unable to tell him how to escape the endless cycles of reincarnations common to the Hindu thought forms of his day. Next, Gautama tried a life of extreme self-denial, existing, it is written, on one grain of rice per day. His physical body in the process was reduced to almost a skeleton. At this stage the seeker decided that extreme self-denial and intellectual training were to no avail. They simple emaciated both body and mind, instead of leading to enlightenment. Next, the man soon to be the "Buddha" tried intense meditation. One day later he fell down an exhausted man under a tree. After a twenty-four-hour period of intense meditation, he became the "Enlighted One," or the "Buddha." He later wrote of this life-changing experience:

And in me emancipated there
arose the knowledge of my
emancipation. I realized
that destroyed is rebirth,
the religious life has been
led, done is what was to be
there is nought beyond this
world.... Ignorance was dispelled, knowledge arose.
Darkness was dispelled...
light arose. So it is with
him who abide vigilant,
strenuous and resolute. [1]

The fig tree under which this enlightenment occured has been known since as the "Bo" tree, or "Tree of Enlightenment."

With this newfound enlightened knowledge, the "Buddha" gathered a group of five disciples and began in a quiet way what was to be a protest against the ritualism and caste system of the Hinduism he saw as in need of reforming.

Following the conversion of the first five disciples, the movement grew rapidly. At first most of the converts were from the wealthy young nobility class, just as Gautama had been. The first sixty he sent out as missionaries to most of India and Nepal. The last forty years of his life, the "Buddha" lived as a monk in Nepal and northern India. An insight into his last years comes from this report:

When the evening was come,
it was his custom to receive
any of his disciples who had
come to see him from a distance, giving them counsel
and advise, and clearing up
any difficulties they might
have, so that he sent them
away cheered and strengthened.
The evening being now far
advanced and feeling cramped

---

[1] Edward J. Thomas, *The Life of Buddha as Legend and History* (New York: Alfred A. Knopf, 1922) p. 68.

with so much sitting, the
Buddha would spend some time
in just pacing up and down to
relieve his legs until it
was time for him to retire
to his rooms for the night.[2]

The original Buddha was eighty when he died at Kusinara near the Himalayas. Contrary to his wished his followers began to worship him as a person rather than as a teacher, and he soon became a symbol of compassion and self-knowledge.

Two hundred years later Buddhism developed strength in India and spread into Ceylong, China and Japan. The conversion of some Mongol tribes in the sixteenth century, AD, was the last vast territorial gain prior to Buddhism's invasion of the United States.

Buddhist beliefs....

Gautama, the "Buddha," was primarily concerned with the pain and meaninglessness of human life. Therefore, he sought to provide a path to a realm where there is no time, pain or death. He taught that the responsibility for the future was with the individual person. Each person is to work out his own deliverance by escaping from the horrible pain of human existence. This process of redemption consists of removing deception from life. A selection from a Buddhist writing called the *Dhammapada* makes this clear:

All that we are is the
result of what we have thought:
it is founded on our thoughts
.... If a man speaks or acts
with an evil thought, pain
follows him.... Hatred does
not cease by hatred at any
time; hatred ceases by love
.... Carpenters fashion wood;
wise people fashion themselves.[3]

The route of redemption according to Buddha is commonly referred to as "The Four Noble Truths." They are:

1) Natural human existence is filled with Dukkah, or "pain, anxiety, frustration." The first step in deliverance is an acknowledgement of that fact. The truth simply states that suffering is everywhere and involved in the very nature of life. It is so bound up with individual human existence that is makes of life a series of suffering experiences.

2) The cause of this pain is Samudaya, or "false craving for and attachment to this world. In essence, then, suffering is caused by an inner craving for individual ego which cannot be satisfied ultimately.

3) This pain can be stopped. Suffering ceases when desire ceases. A state of genuine peace is found only when human passions have been completely extinguished.

[2]C.H.S. Ward, *Buddhism,* Volume I (London: Epworth Press, 1948) pp. 44-45.

[3]*The World's Great Religions,* (New York: Golden Press, Ind., 1967) p. 37.

4) The 8-Fold Path constitutes the fourth truth. This path consists of eight aspects of life which must be kept in proper perspective. It is a kind of course in disciplined self-imporvement leading to the extinction of man's desires and resulting in moral perfection. This path the "Buddha" called "The Middle Way", avoiding the two extremes of self-indulgence and self-mortification, both of which Gautama had tested and found wanting.

The eight steps in this path are:

1) Right mind-set or viewpoint. This involves an utter rejection of incorrect philosophical positions about such important matters as the self and its destiny and of unworthy or unethical attitudes, which may result in covetousness, lying or gossip.

2) Right aspiration, based on happiness and compassion as being life's true values. This involves also freeing one's thoughts from such things as lust and cruelty.

3) Right speech, coming from a proper attitude toward others and, therefore, controlled and considerate. One must refrain from lying, and harsh or vain talk. Words should be gentle, soothing, penetrating to the heart, useful, rightly timed and according to the facts.

4) Right behavior, avoiding any retaliatory actions or even the harboring of resentment. This also includes charity and abstention from killing any living being or embryo. Stealing and unlawful sexual intercourse are also condemned.

5) Right livelihood, forbidding any involvement in any business which might injure any form of life. Each one must take up work which will give scope to his abilities and make him useful to his fellow-man.

6) Right effort, which includes a chosen rate of growth, determined by each individual based on his own situation. This growth comes in four basic areas: The effort to avoid evil, to overcome evil, to develop conditions such as concentration and rapture and then maintain and bring to maturity and protection those good conditions which may already exist. The result of this right effort will be universal love.

7) Right mindfulness, the four aspects of which are: The contemplation of the changeableness and loathesome condition of the body, the contemplation of the feelings of oneself and others, the contemplation of the mind and the contemplation of phenomena with the goal of the complete mastery of one's mental processes.

8) Right concentration, or a complete singleness of mind-set. It can lead into travels where the devotee is purified from all distractions and evils and is filled with rapture and bliss. Finally, he passes beyond sensation of either pleasure or pain into a state going beyond consciousness, ultimately attaining full enlightenment, which is the highest possible state of perfection.

This is the way for Buddha. One sees here a combination of morality, concentration and enlightenment which consists in the long spiritual journey leading at last to Buddhahood.

The founder of Buddhism also prescribed six guidelines for monks who are to be his followers. The guidelines forbid: partaking of intoxicating liquors; partaking of food after midday; being present at any dramatic, dancing or musical performance; using any personal adornment or perfumes; or sleeping on a broad, comfortable bed or owning any gold or silver.

The purpose of the following of the eightfold path is the reaching of Nirvana for the individual Buddhist. Nirvana is the complete opposite of pain. It is a deathless state of mind. For the Buddhist this is the ultimate or the eternal. Nirvana for the Buddhist is a ethical state, a condition which elminate the necessity for any future rebirth. It is the cessation of becoming.

Perhaps the most unique contribution Buddhism has made to the world's religions is Anatta, or "no self, no soul." According to Buddhist teachings, persons have no inner identity this being taken to mean a separate identity throughout eternity. a person finds happiness only after he is no longer there. The reaching of Nirvana is therefore the negation of seeing oneself as having ultimate value. Separate individual existence is really an illusion, because the self has no beginning or ending, is eternally changing and possesses only a phenomenal existence. There is nothing eternal or immortal about any person or any part of him.

According to Buddhist thought, the individual is composed of five factors: physical form, feeling, awareness, mental formations and consciousness. The idea of Anatta is built on two propositions:

1) Nothing in reality corresponds to such words or ideas as "I," "mine" or "belonging."
2) Nothing in our personality is worthy of being regarded as the real self.

In other words, every day the Buddhist is taught to behave as if there is no "I."

The question as to whether Buddhism is atheistic has been debated for centuries. Buddhism can be called atheistic because it denies the existence of the Creator or any being who stands outside human beings and the world. Buddhists also deny any personal power who judges the actions of persons.

However, from Hinduism, Buddhism continues to recognize the law of *Karma*. This law conveys the principle that a person's willed actions produce future mental and physical results in keeping with their original quality. Thus, Karma's twin is rebirth and neither is understandable without the other. This makes the law of cause and effect an unbroken chain throughout the ages.

The doctrine of rebirth accounts for differences at birth which Buddhists attribute neither to chance, environment nor Creator.

So, Buddhists are atheistic in the denial of an ultimate personal being called God. However, the principle of accountability remains.

When the original Buddha taught that *metta* (compassion) should be the guide for relations with others, he lifted Indian ethics to a new level. However, metta stops with empathetic identity and has little of the active justice which predominates the Judaeo-Christian ethic.

Buddhism's heritage of beliefs shows a combination of reliance on Hindusim in such matters as Karma, combined with a reformed emphasis on morality. This combination is stressed in the following proverb:

All desires should be abandoned,
But if you cannot abandon the,
Let your desire be for you salvation.
That is the cure for it....
An excellent man, like precious metal,
Is in every way invarible;
A villian, like a scale,
Is always varing, upwards and downwards. [4]

Buddhist Literature....

The writings in Buddhism may be divided in one of two ways. They may be divided between *Dharma* and *Vinaya*. *Dharma* deals with literature which deals with beliefs. *Vinaya* deals with disciplinary matters for monks.

Buddhist literature may also be divided between *Sutra* and *Shasta*. A *Sutra* is a text which claims to have been spoken by the original Buddha. A *Shastra* is a document written by an author who tries to make commentary on the *Sutras*.

The scriptures of Buddhism which have survived to the present may be divided into three collections: the *Pali Tripitaka*, the *Chinese Tripitaka* ("Three Baskets") and the Tibetan *Kanjur*. These collections are joined by a number of works written in Sanskrit which are not so easily cataloged.

Buddhist Sects....

Buddhism is most clearly and commonly divided between two large schools, the Hinayana ("small raft") and the Mahayana ("large raft"). Hinayanists prefer to call their sect, "The Way of the Elders," or *Theravada*.

In order to remember the distinctives of the two groups, the students may find this chart useful:

HINAYANA	MAHAYANA
Sutras	Shastras
Arhat (monk)	
Srilanka, Burma and Thailand	Korea, Japan, USA and Tibet
Conservative	Liberal
Gautama Buddha	Bodhisattva
Thin Buddha	Fat Buddha
Individual	Community

In order to capture the spirit of the differences between the two groups and to understand why they are called Hinayana ("small raft") and Mahayana ("large raft") respectievely, one should close his eyes after reading this paragraph and imagine these two scenes:

You are standing beside a wide flowing river in the flood
stage. In the middle of the river you spot a small boat with
one man aboard, standing erect. You signal for help, but are
ignored as the boat passes. A few minutes later comes

---

[4]*The World's Great Religions,* op. cit., p. 54.

another boat, almost as wide as the river with hundreds of smiling people on board. You signal for help and are immediately assisted.

This first boat symbolizes Hinayana or Theravada Buddhism. The ideal is the monk, with an austere self-denial and individualistic approach toward questing after Nirvana. Only the *Sutras*, or original sayings of Buddha are to be consulted and followed in determining ethical and theological issues. The original Buddha remains the model and is pictured as thin, unsmiling and resolute in most Theravada Buddhist art. Hinayana Buddhism is also called Southern Buddhism and predominates in Sri Lanka, Cambodia, Burma and Thailand.

The second boat symbolizes Mahayana Buddhism. Mahayanists regard the *Shastras*, or commentaries on the *Sutras* as being almost on a par with the original sayings of Buddha. They do constitute for them sacred literature. Mahayanists do not emulate and idealize the work, but have respect for the *Boddhisattva*, a term referring to one who has attained his own salvation but voluntarily renounces it out of compassion for his fellow humans whom he actively seeks to lead to salvation, even though it may require countless rebirths. The *Bodhisattva* is so in empathy (Metta) with the sufferings of all human beings that he refuses to enter into Nirvana until all others can enter with him. One outstanding *Bodhisattva* is the goddess of mercy, Kwan-yin, who has taken a vow of mercy to help anyone who needs it to attain Nirvana.

The Mahayanists therefore stress the community effort to achieve Nirvana. They are not nearly so individualistic as are their counterpart, the Hinayanists.

Buddha is pictured in Mahayana-dominated settings as the fat, jolly Buddha most westerners are family with.

It should be noted that Hinayanists and Mahayanists, in spite of their differences, do hold certain truths in common. They are:
1) Moderation as a way of life.
2) Overcoming evil with good and love;
3) Anger, envy, and jealousy are the roots of evil;
4) The unmaking of self through wisdom;
5) Life as ever fleeting or disappearing.

Thus, both Mahayanists and Hinayanists are Buddhists with common beliefs, but being almost as dissimilar as similar in actual life-style.

A third sect has proven popular in Japan and deserves attention here. This "Pure Land" School is loosely a part of Mahayana, but belongs in a category of its own, largely because of its emphasis on salvation by faith. This school proclaims the "easy way" to the Pure Land by a simple recitation of the sacred formula which expresses faith in the Amida Buddha. The ideal is *Amida Buddha*, the "Buddha of Infinite Light and Life." He, having reached the threshold of enlightenment on the basis of hard-earned merit as a being in past lives, vowed not to enter Buddhahood until the entrance to the Pure Land he established could be assured for all beings simply because they rely on him and his name. All persons without distinction may be assured of eternal happiness on the basis of faith in *Amida* and reliance on his sacred vow which is expressed by reciting, "Hail Amida Buddha." With this assurance, the adherent is expected to live a life of joy, gratitude and good works.

Tibetan Buddhism stands in a category all its own, as well, although it may be placed under the heading of Mahayana. When Buddhism was introduced into Tibet in the seventh century, AD, it was mixed with magic as a means of coping with life. Even today Tibetan Buddhists frequently carry *Tantras* or manuals that teach the magical words and spells that help one deal with the evil unknown. For that reason, Tibetan Buddhism is sometimes called *Tantric* Buddhism.

Tibetan Buddhism is also marked by its use of the prayer wheel, a cylinder containing prayers and ritual incantations. Within this cylinder is an agitator, which when turned, stirs up the written prayers and they are "prayed" by that motion. They may even be set up as water wheels at streams and be "prayed" as the water flows.

Tibetan Buddhism is also known by its clergy, called *Lamas*, or "superior ones." The *Lamas* have long been divided into two orders, the "Yellow Hats" and the "Red Hats." The *Dalai* ("sea") *Lama* comes from the larger of the two schools, the "Yellow Hats." He is seen as the ruler of Tibet. When one dies, a search is made over Tibet by "Yellow Hat" monks for a male child who has the qualities of the deceased *Dalai*. Then the boy begins a long period of training designed to prepare him for the leadership of the Tibetan peoples.

In 1950, Tibet was invaded by China. In 1959, a young *Dalai Lama* led a revolution against their Chinese conquerors, but was defeated and fled to India. Under Communist control, the *Dalai Lama* tradition suffers in modern Tibet.

Buddhism in the United States....

Chinese Mahayana Buddhism reached Japan five centuries after Christ, having come through Korea. In the past generation, Mahayana Buddhism came from Japan to the United States. The major divisions in the United States follow the three major sects of Mahayana Buddhism found in Japan:
1) The "Pure Land" sects;
2) The intuitive or meditative sects, as in Zen
3) The "Socio-political" symbolized by Soka Gakkai.
In addition, the United States has seen the influx of Tibetan, or Tantric Buddhism, especially in the 1970's.

The "Pure Land" sects are called Jodo and Shingon in Japan. In the United States, they have taken the form of the Buddhist Churches of America, an organization presently publishing a series of tracts, a newsletter and a monthy leaflet, "The American Buddhist." In some respects, these Buddhists are much like American Protestants. For example, there is a strong educational and social emphasis because the organization follows the "Pure Land" idea that it is not necessary to withdraw from the world to become a perfect Buddhist.

The Buddhist Churches of America has in 1978 about eighty

churches and a membership of almost fifty thousand in the United States.

The problem of cultural adaptation involved with establishing "Pure Land" Buddhism in the United States is reflected in an editorial in "The American Buddhist":

Wither American Buddhism? Is our Buddhism actually American Buddhism? Can we apply Buddhist teachings in promoting and enriching our American way of life?.... American Buddhists are making a sincere attempt to present Buddhism to meet our American needs. This trend is truly encouraging....[5]

The "Pure Land" sect of Buddhism seems to have found a permanent home in America through the American Buddhist Churches. To survive, its adherents must continue to struggle with the question of relating a basically Japanese religion to American culture.

The most militant and flourishing company of Buddha's followers in the United States is the Nichiren Shoshu Association, or as it is known in Japan, Sokagakai. (An entire chapter is given to it in this book.)

Zen is by far the most popular form of Zen meditation in the United States. Its practice often cuts across lines of religious preference. As a means of deliverance from material concern and as a device of experiencing everyday beauty, Zen has a broad appeal in the United States. In 1930, the Zen Institute in America was founded. The institute currently publishes two monthly leaflets, "Zen Notes" and "Letters from Kyoto." A Zen monastery is in the mountains of California near the Tassajara Hot Springs. It is called the "Zen Mountain Center" and is run by the Zen Center in San Francisco, which publishes *Wind Bell*, a monthly publication which tells of the monastery and the practice of Zen. The Zen Center's director says there are more potential students of Zen in America than in Japan. He may be right! (See chapter in this book on Zen.)

Tantric Buddhism, a Tibetan transplant, is also growing in popularity in America. All of the major sects of Tibetan Buddhism have established meditation centers in the United States.

One Tibetan monk is Chogyam Trungpa, born in Tibet in 1939. He came to the United States in 1970 to found "The Tail of the Tiger" Community near Barnet, Vermont. It is a meditation center and spiritual training ground for his disciples.

Trungpa states that in his Buddhist meditation practice, "The concept of nowness plays an important part. Whatever one does...is not aimed at achieving a higher state or at following some theory or ideal but simply...trying to see what is here and now."[6]

Trungpa dislikes, however, the guru role. He says that encouraging Americans to try to behave like Tibetans is a hindrance to their spiritual development because it encourages them to remain attached

---

[5]Laverne S. Sasaki, "Whether American Buddhism?" in *The American Buddhist*, Vol. II, number 4, April, 1967, p. 1.

[6]Chogyam Trungpa, *Meditation in Action* (Berkeley: Shambala, 1970) p. 51

to externals. He will continue to stress meditation, Buddhist style, to those whose spirits can hear.

Buddhism is attracting substantial numbers of Americans in at least four forms. Inroads are being made rapidly into non-Oriental Americans, a sure sign of Buddhism's status as truly a world religion.

Conclusion....

It is a long way from Benares, India, to Vermont. This length of that journey is symbolic of the wide appeal of the teachings of the "Buddha." He found enlightenment and since then to have others in his school. The future of Buddhism is a bright one as weary beings took for escape from pain and anxiety.

BIBLIOGRAPHY

Edward Conze, *Buddhism? Its Essence and Development.* (New York: Harper and Row, 1959)

Richard A. Gord, *Buddhism.* (Englewood Cliffs, New Jersey) Prentice -Hall, 1961)

Christmas Humphreys, *Exploring Buddhism* (London: Allen and Unwin, 1974)

Kenneth Scott Latourette, *Introducing Buddhism* (New York: Friendship Press, 1963)

D.T. Suzuki, *The Essence of Buddhism* (New York: International Publications, Service, 1968)

Naji Wara:
My name is Naji Wara and I am a thirty-year-old resident of Osaka, Japan. I am the father of three boys and employed at an auto assembly plant as a line supervisor.

In my teen years I was exposed to "Pure Land" Amida Buddhism. Since that time I have been happy and my family and I are pleased with the peace we know.

The Amida Buddha awaits for me at the "Pure Land" entrance and he refuses to enter that paradise until I get there. There is something comforting about a Savior figure like this. In gratitude my family and I are engaged in counseling and working with retired employees of the auto plant where I work. It is my eldest son of whom I am proudest at the moment. He has just been awarded a summer camp scholarship where he will study more about our Amida Buddhism.

Phenom:

My name is Phe-nom. I am a nineteen-year-old resident of saigon. I was born in North Vietnam in 1959, just when the French were leaving.

When I was sixteen it was my pleasure to enter a Buddhist monastery near Saigon. It has been my ambition all my life to be a arhat, or monk, the men with shaved heads and beautiful robes begging for their daily meals. My father was a very faithful Buddhist before he was killed in 1973. My mother lives alone now.

In no uncertain terms I have learned that life is filled with Dukkah. It surely is logical to me that some of our monks burned themselves in protest to the war.

My favorite daily activity is the study of the Sutras, the sayings of the original Buddha. At the moment, I am headed toward the enlightenment he knew in perfection.

Chapter IX

Zen

It is maintained by the purists in Zen that to attempt to describe Zen is to do it injustice. Tales abound of Zen teachers who travel six hundred miles to sit silently before a group of Zen disciples, or to clap a pair of hands, ask a riddle or wash a bowl. Zen purists say that Zen must be experienced to be known, not described to be lost in verbosity.

Zen priests also maintain that this school of enlightenment is not attached or indebted to Buddhism or any other religious tradition, but stands on its own.

At the risk of offending such purists, this attempts an insightful if fleeting glimpse at this important and popular discipline.

Zen is almost impossible to define because it shuns the expression of reality in any ideas or concepts. Zen insists that ultimate truth can only be known intuitively. The goal is enlightenment (satori) which usually, but not necessarily, comes through meditation under the direction of a Zen master, or roshi.

If Zen dare be expressed in a philosophical manner, let a Zen teacher do it. Says one Mrs. Ruth Fuller Sasaki:

> Zen holds that there is no god outside the universe who has created it and created man.... Each of us is but a cell as it were, in the body of the Great Self, a cell that comes into being, performs its functions, and passes away, transformed into another manifestation. Though we have temporary individuality, that temporary, limited individuality is not either a true self or our true self. Our true self is the Great Self.[1]

Zen is usually presented as spontaneity. The more effort placed into it, the less likely one is to find enlightenment in Zen. In spite of Zen's shunning of planned achievement and emphasis on spontaneity, Zen is *hard* at least ways, as pointed out by Archie J. Bahm:

1) Zen is *hard* to get into. One cannot will, or reason, or work his way into Zen. Zen will never offer enlightenment as a deserved reward.

2) Zen is *hard* to stay in. A Zen practitioner has to develop skill in retaining Zen and resisting total revitalization of intellect, will, morality and ego.

---

[1] Ruth Fuller Sasaki, "Zen: A Method for Religious Awakening," *The World of Zen: An East-West Anthology* edited by Nancy Wilson Ross, (New York: Random House, 1960) p. 18.

3) Zen is also *hard* because one may, without knowing it, already be in Zen, just as one in Zen may slip away without noticing it.[2]

Confused? Good! Now you are on your way to understanding (or is it not understanding?) Zen.

Is Zen Buddhism? The question of whether Zen is a branch of Buddhism is an open one. Most adherents of Zen maintain that the original (Gautama) Buddha lives on Buddhism as the highest, most perfectly enlightened one, who through his mystic vision gained supreme knowledge. In this way he serves as a model for Zen.

Historically, there are direct ties between Zen and classic Buddhism. Therefore, Zen may be defined as, "That school of enlightenment born from the mystical stream in Buddhism."

The spread of Buddhism from its native India to China ranks as one of the major events in the entire history of world religions. Without that spread, there would be little Japanese or American Buddhism today.

When the Chinese heard the Sanskrit word "Dhyana," they called it "Chan." In Japan, it became "Zen" where its original meaning of "ceremonial release" was retained. Zen can be traced to classic Buddhism, as demonstrated below.

History....

During the first great period of Chinese Buddhism, the most brilliant representative was Seng-Chao (384-414 AD). He was oriented to the immediate experiential perception of absolute truth. Seng-Chao saw that truth as revealing itself through *paradox* as the means of expressing the inexpressible. He taught that the inscrutable is found in an intuitive experience, which affords insight into the Oneness of Illision and Reality. This clever combination of Taoist and Buddhist concepts made Seng-Chao's views believable to both camps.

However, the person generally regarded as the founder of Zen was Tao-cheng (360-434 AD.) He was born in a monastery where he was exposed constantly to a synthesis of Taoism and Buddhism. He was taught that the Buddha equals the Tao. Tao-cheng gave preference to sudden illumination, which he modeled after the original Buddha.

During this period, the Zen poem, an integral part of Zen in the modern world, was developed. The following one may have been written by Tao-cheng himself:

> A special tradition outside the scriptures;
> No dependence upon words and letters;
> Direct pointing at the soul of man;
> Seeing into one's own nature; and
> The attainment of Buddhahood.

As one can see from this early Zen poem, an early emphasis was a lack of dependency on external stimuli for obtaining enlightenment.

---

[2]Archie J. Bahm, *The World's Living Religions* (New York: Dell Publishing Co., 1964) p. 210f.

According to Tao-cheng, the experience of enlightenment should come suddenly.

Bodhiharma is the key figure of the second stage of Zen growth in China. Reliable facts about his life are few. There are even those who argue that he never existed in fact, but was created as an ideal. Legend states that he was once seated for nine years without interruption, staring at a blank wall. One supposed historical event in Bodihiharam's life was his encounter with the Emperor Wu-Ti, where he asserted the futility of building Buddhist temples and of recitation of the *Sutras*.

Bodhiharma was followed by Hui-neng (638-713 AD), a mendicant who gave much impetus to modern Zen. He argued that Zen is built on the view of an absolute monism; i.e., there is but one reality. He said this in a famous four-line poem:

The Bodhi is not like a tree,
    The clear mirror is nowhere standing.
    Fundamentally not one thing exists;
    Where, then, is a grain of dust to cling?

Hui-neng taught that this one reality is Spirit, which he also equated with mind. He presented Zen's goal as to be freed from all duality in order that the mind may exist in purity. A well-known saying of Hui-neng's, "To take refuge by the mind in one's nature is to take refuge in the true Buddha."

The Zen master, Dogen (1200-1253 AD) did more than any other one person to bring Zen recognition in Japan. He stressed the changableness of all things. It is for Zazen that Dogen is best known. Zazen is the meditative in which the disciple sits upright with legs crossed. By doing Zazen, the disciple is to reach the state of concentration in which he is aware of both thinking and not-thinking and yet is limited by neither.

Next to Dogen, Hakuin (1685-1768 AD) was the greatest Zen master of the modern era. He is important because he chronicled his enlightenment experiences. In his valuable records, he describes two phases of the enlightenment process: "great tension" in which the mind is under pressure to the point of explosion and the "solution" in an estatic experience of released enlightenment. This helped to make it clear that there are degrees and stages to satori, or enlightenment.

The greatest interpreter of Zen to the western world in the twentieth century has been D.T. Suzuki, author of *An Introduction to Zen Buddhism* and *A Manual of Zen Buddhism.* (See bibliography at the end of this chapter). Dr. Suzuki was professor of Buddhist Philosophy at Otani University in Kyoto, Japan.

D.T. Suzuki's primary strength was his ability to phrase Zen in concepts readily understandable to Americans interested in Zen. Some examples are:

1) The foundation of all concepts is simple, unsophisticated experience.

2) The ordinary logical process of reasoning is powerless to give final satisfaction to our deepest spiritual needs.

3) To be free, life must be an absolute affirmation.

4) The Koan (Zen riddle) has as its objective the arousing of doubt and pushing doubt to its furthest limits. [3]

Zen continues to reach into the modern American Christian camp through such articulate interprepers as D.T. Suzuki. Among the most famous of such Christian devotees was Thomas Merton, who died at a Buddhist-Christian dialogue meeting. Father Merton wrote in *Conjectures of a Guilty Bystander:*

> The atheist existentialist has my respect, he accepts his honest despair with Stoic dignity. And, despair gives his thought a genuine content, because it expresses an experience, his confrontation with emptiness.... We believe not because we want to know, but because we want to *be*. [4]

Former Episcopal priest Alan Watts has had more influence on American youth than any other person in the past generation. It was he who taught American youth such phrases as, "Do your own thing", "It's not my bag", "Cool it", "Whatever turns you on" and "Celebrate" through popularizing classic Zen concepts. This is partly because Watts was able to relate Zen to an audience with Judaeo-Christian presupositions. He did so by such statements as:

> The appeal of Zen is that it unveils behind the urgent realm of good and evil a vast region of oneself about which there need be no guilt or recrimination, where at last the self is indistinguishable from God. But the Westerner who is attracted to Zen and who must understand it deeply must have one indispensable qualification: he must understand his own culture so thoroughly that he is no longer swayed by its premises unconsciously. [5]

Zen has had and continues to have its outstanding practioners and spokesmen, both from a classic Buddhist and mystical Christian perspective. The future of Zen is as difficult to predict as Zen itself is to define, but it will probably continue to appeal to mysitcs in all traditions.

One reason Zen grows in the United States is the American Zen Center with a retreat near Tassajara, California. Dozens of Americans come there to study Zen for a day or a year. A regular publication is *The Wind Bell*, containing poems and prose designed to make more interested in Satori through Zen. The center is headed by a former Christian minister from Texas who turned his evangelistic efforts toward those who would know reality outside good and evil warfare.

Here is Zen....

Zen can be an instantaneous awareness inspired by a perplexing conversation with a teacher:

> "I have no peace of mind, please pacify my mind", said the student.

---

[3] D. T. Suzuki, *An Introduction to Zen Buddhism.* (New York: Grove Press, 1964).

[4] Thomas Merton, *Conjectures of a Guilty Bystander* (Garden City, N.Y.: Image Books, 1966) p. 87.

[5] Alan Watts, "Beat Zen, Square Zen and Zen", *The World of Zen,* op. cit., p. 334.

"Bring out your mind here and I will pacify it," replied the teacher.

"But when I seek my own mind I cannot find it," said the student.

"There, I have pacified your mind," said the teacher.

Zen may be abandoning all efforts, as in this poem:

When one looks at it,
one cannot see it.
When one listens for it,
One cannot hear it.
But when uses it, it is inexhaustible.

Zen may be the sudden experience of Satori:

ZTT! I entered.

Zen may be a living awareness of all of life being a part of one reality:

I raise my hand. I see the clouds blow away beyond the neighboring words. I am living Zen.

Zen may be ceasing to struggle over one of the 1700 classic Zen Koans or riddles:

"Who is the Buddha?" asked a student.
"The cat climbed the post," answered his roshi.

Or, Zen may be responding to Zen in the arts, such as short unrhymed Haikus, or poems:

My but in spring!
True, there is nothing in it,
There is everything.

Conclusion....

A famous Zen cartoon shows a monk warming himself on a cold day. For his firewood he has chopped up a statue of the Buddha. He is shown raising his robe and warming his backside by the fire. The warm backside is more important than any trappings of religion. He is living Zen. He hears the sound of one hand clapping — because he has stopped listening for it.

BIBLIOGRAPHY

Thomas Merton, *Conjectures of a Guilty Bystander* (Garden City, N.Y.: Image Books 1966)

D.T. Suzuki, *A Manual of Zen Buddhism* (New York: Grove Press, Inc. 1960)

D.T. Suzuki, *An Introduction to Zen Buddhism* (N.Y., Grove Press, 1964)

Alan Watts, Psychotherapy: *East and West* (N.Y.: Ballantine Books, 1972)

Nancy Wilson Ross (editor) *The World of Zen: an East-West Anthology* (New York: Random House, 1960)

Fuji:
(The following is the testimonial of Fuji, a sixty-year-old Zen roshi who resides in Japan):

Marty:
My name is Marty. I am twenty-four years old and have been in the army for two years. While on duty in Japan, I got introduced to Zen. Since that time, I have known Satori but once. It was an indescribable experience of oneness with all reality.

The Koans have helped a lot because I used to go at religion like I go at all life, with firm resolve to find some kind of answer to every question. With Zen, I found that *being* is more important than performing on any level. Freedom to be, that's what it's all about with Zen.

You asked me to explain Zen. It can't be done. It can only be experienced. To begin, you might try sitting quietly for twelve hours or just go wash your bowls.

Chapter X

Shinto

Shinto has been defined as "the traditional religious practices which originated in Japan and developed mainly among the Japanese people along with the underlying life attitudes and ideology which support such practices."[1]

The origins of Shinto lie in the hazy sea mists of the dawn of Japanese history. This is so much the case that by the time the Japanese people got to defining and crystallizing their beliefs and practices were already with them.

Brief history....

The ancient Japanese peoples were familar with a feeling of awe and mystery in the presence of the unknown. This gave early rise to the development of a type of nature-worship combined with clan mores. Before effected by Chinese intrusion, in the forms of Confucianism in cultural etiquette, Taoism with its emphasis on flowing with nature, and Buddhism with its rigid negativism, Shinto was undeveloped and naive. Like most ainism, early Shinto made few distinctions, as being living and unliving beings, the sacred and the secular, and living gods and forces of nature.

Early Shinto religious rites were performed by clan priests and were basically related to agricultural concerns. They were designed to please the kami, or gods, in order that they might look with favor on the crop grower struggling for survival.

One clan won out over the others in early Japanese history. They were the Yamatos, and had one supreme kami known as Amatesura Omikami, the "sun goddess."

In the fifth and sixth centuries, AD, and the influx of Chinese cultural values and patterns, the Yamato Chieftain became an "emperor" in the Chinese tradition. This he was able to mix with the role of priest in the clan ritual. These are the early signs of the emperor (Chinese) being seen as kami, or god (Japanese).

The earlier Shinto also fell under the influence of Chinese Buddhism, with its emphasis on ceremonial forms, developed thoughts on human existence and priestly orders. The disorganized Shinto, still found among the various clans, meshed with Chinese values and Buddhist emphasis to form a hybrid system of belief and practice.

---

[1]"The Character of Shinto Viewed from a History of Religion Perspective," *Encounter* May, 1969, p. 40.

The "writing" period of Japanese history came in the eighth century, AD, with the sacred scriptures, *Nihongi* and *Kojiki* appearing in written form.

In the Heian period (794-1183 AD) Buddhism and Shinto were closely associated. Buddhist names were given to Shinto kami.

The Kamakura period (1185-1333) saw the Shinto priests of the sacred shrine at Ise who attempted to place the Shinto kami in a place of superiority over the Buddhist concepts. It was a call back to an indigenous appreciation for ancient Japanese values.

This laid the foundation for a more pronounced Shinto renewal during the Tokugawa period (1600-1868). Ironically, while Shinto was gaining official and local support, Confucianism began to form the basis of ideology behind the feudel regime.

This Confucian influence led to movement among Shinto priests to purge Shinto of its foreign elements. By now, this was an impossible task. One scholar, Mabuchi (1697-1769), joined others in trying to return Japanese popular religion to its pre-Chinese state. This was mixed with a fervent nationalistic spirit.

The Samurai warriors cannot be overlooked as a part of the Japanese life during the Tokugawa period. They lived with a combined Shinto-Confucianist warrior code called BuShido. Reflective of this code are these emphases:

1) The samurai is bound to be loyal to his master in the feudal system heirarchy.
2) He is to exhibit great courage.
3) He is to be a man of honor.
4) He is to be polite to his master.
5) He is to be a cultured gentleman in every sense of the word.

Suicide was permitted to the Samurai as a way of avoiding dishonor. This "belly-splitting" suicide was called seppuku.

A.B. Mitford, an official in the British consulate in Japan more than a century ago, witnessed a ritual suicide. His report reads in part:

The condemned man was Taki Zenzaburo...a stalwart man, thirty-two years of age...who advanced slowly toward the Japanese witnesses, and...bowed before them....

Bowing once more, the condemned man allowed his upper garments to slip down to his girdle, and remained naked to the waist. Carefully, according to custom, he tucked his sleeves under his knees to prevent himself from falling forwards. Deliberately, with a steady hand, he took the dirk (a short sword with a razor edge); he looked at it wistfully, almost affectionately; for a moment seemed to collect his thoughts for the last time and then, stabbing himself deeply below the waist on the left-hand side, he drew the dirk slowly across the waist to the right side, and, turning in the wound, gave a slight cup upwards. During this sickeningly painful operation, he never moved a muscle of his face. When he drew out the dirk, he leaned forward and stretched out his neck; an expression of pain for the first time crossed his face, but he uttered no sound. At that moment, the Kaishaku (second) who, still crouching by his side, had been keenly watching his every movement, sprang to his feet, poised his sword for a second in the air; there was a flash, a heavy, ugly thud, a crashing fall; with one blow the head had been severed from the body. [2]

A dead silence followed.... It was horrible.

In 1868, a major change took place in Japanese history. The emperor Meiji took office as a powerful ruler with a religio-nationalistic base. The emperor, again regarded as kami, set up a special department of Shinto. Shinto was now officially the Japanese religion. Priests were paid by the government and local shrines were supported, in effect, by federal tax money.

A separation was made, however, between "State" Shinto and "Sect" Shinto. Thirteen carefully selected "sects" of Shinto were chosen as free to express traditional Japanese *religious* values. State Shinto was officially declared not in the "religious" realm. The persons representing State Shinto were assigned the upkeep of the shrines, centers of patriotic rather than religious rituals. All Japanese were required to participate regularly at shrines and to submit to government edicts, especially those coming from the empeior, viewed as kami.

Twentieth century Shinto saw its government tie religious and nationalistic concerns to the degree of proposed Japanese worldwide denomination.

In 1946, after much arbitration, it was declared that the Emperor was not divine. Allied leaders presided over the disolution of official state Shinto. However, this dissolution has not been successful. The 1978 Japanese yearbook lists more than 75,000,000 adherents of all Shinto bodies of bothe "Shrine" and "Sect" categories, about seventy percent of the current Japanese population.

Basic beliefs....

The Japanese mythology upon which modern Shinto belief is based is found primarily in two eighth century, A.D. books. They are the *Kojiki* ("Records of Ancient Matters") and the *Nihongi* ("Chronicles of Japan.")

In these works, creation is described as beginning with a spontaneous generation of an original kami trio:
1) "The Lord who fills heaven"
2) Two other kami related the fertility.

The last of the kami created were Izanagi and Izanami. This male-female team stirred up the sea with a spear. When the spear came up out of the water, the drops of water from it formed an island network.

Izanami was fatally burned while giving birth to the kami of fire and departed from the earth into the realm of the dead.

Susano O, in the tradition of the storm-god, originated from the cleansing of Izanagi's nose. She is a destructive entity who does

---

[2]A. D. Mitford, *Tales of Old Japan*. (London: Macmillan, 1871), pp. 235-236.

things contrary to the mores of an agricultural community and to the sense of purity of ceremony. Susano O so offended her sister, the sun goddess, Anaterasa, that the latter withdrew into a cave in heaven, leaving the world in darkness. In despair, all the other kamis got together to try to bring the sun goddess and her heavenly sunshine back into their lives. She was finally coaxed out of the cave by her own reflection shining in a mirror outside the cave. At that time, Susano O was banished out of heaven into the land of darkness.

The kami function under various identities in these creation accounts. At times, they are identified with natural phenomena, such as islands, the sun and the moon. They often act in human ways, but frequently evidence powers that are beyond human ability. Kami may refer to spiritual beings existing today, mythological entities of ancient times, physical objects of worship or ancestral spirits.

Man is seen as basically good, he must demonstrate that by acting in ways that enhance order and harmony in society. While persons are basically good, they may become impure by mixing with or touching what is polluted. This may include contact with blood, sickness, death, the action of evil spirits or ceremonial laxity. As a result, Shinto ritual is usually more concerned with ceremonial purification of the external body than with an inward cleansing. This brings the student to the subject of Shinto ritual.

Shinto ritual....

Shinto rites vary from simple daily home ceremonies to elaborate ritual at state Shinto shrines on very special occasions.

The home alter is usually of simple construction coming out of the wall in the living room. Before this structure, which is a type of miniature shrine, religious rites are performed.

The shrine is the center of Shinto worship. There the kami are housed and worshipped. It is usually near a wooded area. The entrance is marked by a *torii*, or "bird perch," made of two upright pillars and two cross beams. Along the path to the holy place, there is usually a washing place where the water is provided for purification.

At the shrine, a number of buildings may be present including: an office, priest's quarters, a storehouse, etc. The worshipper usually is not allowed to enter the sanctuary proper. There are no images in the shrine, but a short bamboo rod may symbolize the presence of the kami.

The four elements of Shinto worship are: purification, offering, prayer and a sacred meal.

Purification is usually washing. The offering at the shrine is usually money tossed into the offering box in front of the sanctuary. Prayers are not vocalized by the worshippers and are accompanied by a series of bows and two hand claps, as if to awaken the kami. The sacred meal is held on special occasions as a means of having fellowship with a particular kami, with whom the meal is symbolically shared.

This ritual is particularly heightened on festival days. One of the most important occasions is the Great Purification Ceremony which is performed twice a year, on the last days of June and December. The purpose of this ceremony is to cleanse people and land from the pollution incurred during the previous six months. An ancient prayer is usually prayed by a priest during this ceremony, which reads in part:

Now, the sins committed purposely or otherwise by the people born in this peacefully governed land will be large in number...but such times, in accordance with the laws of the divine land, you must offer the Deities certain things which are good for the world, as atonement for your sins...and you must utter sincere words in repentance....

Know, therefore, that, when cast away thus, all the sins and impurities will be thoroughly purified and cleansed from this day so that any and every one of them will altogether disappear from this world.[3]

All of these rituals are designed to create and reflect an intimate link with the kami. These rites are also created to enable persons to display sincerity, purity and brightness, having completed the ritual. These rituals allow basically good persons to be purified so that they may live a happy life as a helpful member of a happy society.

Modern Shinto....

Modern Shinto may be divided into three basic sects: mountain, shamanism and "pure" Shinto.

The mountain sects of modern Shinto especially revere Ontake and Fuji. A combination of nature worship and self-discipline is exhibited by the hundreds of thousands of Japanese who climb these mountains daily.

The modern shamanistic sects emphasize faith-healing. Tenri-Kyo is called "the Christian Science of Japan." It was founded by Nakayama Miki (1798-1887), who claimed to be possessed by the Kami of Divine Reason. To faith healing the sect adds volunteer labor for public charity.

Those who try to worship in a "pure" Shinto are concerned to preserve the religious traditions of Japan. They also emphasize fasting, breath control and chanting, similar to the Yoga of India.

Conclusion....

In 1946, Shinto was highly fragmented by official decree. However, Shinto continues to exist through such "new religions" in Japan as *Tenri-Kyo*. These have arisen through a period of intense social change and emphasis on economic revival in Japan.

Shinto remains the bedrock of Japanese religion. As it has been influenced by such movements as *Bushido* in the past and *Tenri-Kyo* in the present, it will survive attempts to replace it in the future.

---

[3]Quoted from: Clark B. Offner, "Shinto" in *The World's Religions,* J. N. Anderson, editor (Chicago: Inter-Varsity Press, 1976), 207.

BIBLIOGRAPHY

William T. deBary, (editor) *Sources of the Japanese Tradition* (New York: Columbia University Press, 1958)
Jean Herbert, *Shinto: Fountainhead of Japan* (New York: Stein and Day, 1967)
D.C. Holtom, *The National Faith of Japan* (New York: Paragon, 1965)
Genchi Kato, *A Study of Shinto* (New York: Barnes and Noble, 1971)
Floyd Ross, *Shinto: The Way of Japan* (Boston: Beacon Press, 1965)

Inriki:

My name is Inriki and I live in Tokyo. I am eighteen years old and am a student in the university. Shinto to me is my grandmother's religion. She lives with us. Every day when I arise she is in the living room giving food offerings to the Kami on our god shelf in the livingroom.

I guess the most fun is at special festivals when we all go to the shrine. We pass through the Torii, wash ourself at the stream and watch the priests as they enter the holy place to pray for the pleasing of the kami. Afterwards, we may stay for a meal in which it is said that the kami join us.

When I am married it will be at a Shinto shrine because my father will insist, mainly for the sake of my grandmother. We will dress in black and be pronounced married. When I start my own home, I am not at all sure we will have a god shelf, but we will not miss the festivals.

Fujiwara:

My name is Fujiwara and I am a twenty-year-old worker in a department store in downtown Kyoto. It is at night when I really come alive because it is then that a bunch of guys practice the ancient Japanese warrior code of Bushido. We have a place to work out and we read a lot of books to see how they lived back then.

No one messed with a Bushido warrior. Their samurai swords were sharp and so were their minds. A lot of people think that following Bushido is mainly physical exercise, but it is the way of the cultured gentleman. We study a lot of Chinese and Japanese history to see what we should do. We study healing through such herbs as ginseng and I am learning to play the flute. That may look "sissy" to some but it is part of being Bushido. Oh, yeah, if you think I'm "sissy," just call me that...once!

Chapter XI

Confucianism

Confuciansim is imbedded in the total philosophy and practices of the ancient Chinese. It is so interwoven that there is still an open question in the minds of many scholars as to whether Confucianism is even a religion. After all, Confucianism does lack a priesthood, sacred writings from an "Inspired" perspective, and any doctrine of an afterlife. Nonetheless, Confucianism is an ethical system and deserves attention for this and other reasons that shall become apparent as this chapter emerges.

Confucius....

Kung Fu-tzu, or "Kung, the Sage," was born in 551 BC. China at that time was composed politically of a number of small feudal states, often engaged in clan wars. To Confucius, it appeared as a time of decadent luxury and oppression.

Confucius came from an intellectual, but poor, family in the province of Lu in what is now called Shantung. As a teenager, he set out to learn. He was married at age nineteen, but was not very faithful to his family. He soon divorced his wife and maintained an aloof relationship with his wife and daughter. At age twenty-one, he gathered a small group of disciples around him. His reputation grew fast and he attracted many disciples. They lived with him in his home and occasionally followed him in his travels. He taught them history, government, and divination and other humanities.

At about age fifty, Confucius, after repeated attempts to be heard by government officials, was finally able to gain a minor government position. He was appointed as prime minister by the Duke. Legend has it that Confucius was an ideal leader. The crime rate reportedly dropped to nothing. He was, however, forced to resign by enemies at age fifty-five. For the next dozen years, Confucius was a person without a position. He and his few disciple wandered from place to place. They were jeered at until, at age sixty-seven, another position of honor was given him in the province of Ai. Confucius died in 479 BC and was widely mourned by his followers.

A psycho-biology of Confucius would reveal a person who was pleasant, courteous, modest, self-controlled, i.e., a zealot with a sense of humor.

Basic Beliefs....

The teachings of Confucius can be summarized by describing the "ideal man" from his four standards. They are:

1) *Yi*. This is the way things behave when they act in accordance

with their own nature, all will go well. Nature provides each being with a nature that is self-sufficient and thus as good as it can be.

2) *Jen* is goodwill. It is willingness to do what is best socially. This consists basically in allowing each person to behave according to his own nature. This means not wanting him to be different from what he is.

3) *Li* is propriety, or the appropriate way of giving overt expression to inner attitudes. According to Confucius, the society that lives by Li lives smoothly. One of the Confucian classes, the *Li Chi*, Confucius says:

> What I have learned is this, that of all the things that people live by, Li is the greatest. Without Li, we do not know how to conduct a proper worship of the spirits of the universe; or how to establish the proper status of the king and the ministers, the rulers and the ruled, and the elders and the juniors; or how to establish the moral relationships between the sexes; between parents and children, and between brothers; or how to distinguish the different degrees of relationships in the family. [1]

As one can see from the statement above, there are basic relationships in life. When Li is present in these relationships, the social order operates smoothly. They are:
a) Father to son
b) Older brother to younger brother
c) Husband to wife
d) Elder to junior and
e) Ruler to subject.

So, we have Li as a kind of balance wheel of human conduct, tending to prevent either deficiency or excess, and guiding toward the middle path of socially beneficial conduct. This concept of Li, as imparting a certain rythm and decorum to life has been important in Chinese culture ever since the time of Confucius. It has given the Chinese people some of their most distinguishing characteristics.

4) Chi may be defined as wisdom, which consists in confident living. Chi is an ideal to be learned by degrees. One's assurance grows as he learns more. One learns to deviate less and less from nature's norms. One never for a moment abandons the habit of living with confidence.

The four qualities of the "ideal man" help to highlight the teaching of Kung futzu.

The aim of the practice of these four qualities, for Confucius, was to make gentlemen (chuj-tzu). Although the terms originally meant "sons of rulers," Confucius used it to mean men of noble character.

No view of Confucius' thought is complete without notice of his thoughts on government and the Tao. Confucius understood government in terms of individual rulers, not in terms of institutions. Confucius believed strongly that rulers should exercise moral force, or Te. If men in authority were virtuous, the commoners would feel

---

[1] Li Chi, XXVII.

their love and act the same. Confucius is supposed to have said, "Moral force never dwells in solitude, it will always bring neighbors." For Kungfutzen, the proper aim of all government is the welfare and happiness of *all* the people. Capacity to govern, for him, has no necessary connection with birth, wealth, or position. It depends solely on character and virtue. Instead of studying how to handle lawsuits, according to Kungfutzu we shall all seek to create a society in which lawsuits will not be necessary. He hoped for an enlightened society of learned and cultured persons.

Regarding the Tao, the "Way" for Kungfutzu conveys the meaning of the *truth* to which one is committed. For Kungfutzu, the "Way will be realized when qualities such as sincerity and integrity are pursued by all persons within a society.

Mencius....

No discussion of Confucius is complete without a discussion of his chief disciple and critic, Mencius (372-289 BC). Mencius argued that Confucius Chih (wisdom) may best be understood by Chi, or "morale." This, to Mencius, was derived from a social dependency on other members of a social group.

Also, Mencius was strongly opposed to war. He also taught that citizens have the right to revolt against an unjust government. This Mencius based on an even higher view of man than Confucius had. Mencius was largely responsible for so codefying Confucius teachings that they were welded into a religion.

After Mencius, the Confucian system began to spread and its scholars rose to high government positions. A great tomb was built for Confucius and emperors gave him titles such as "Great Sage." Confucius became the patron saint of scholars and sacrifices were frequently made for him in outstanding centers of higher education in China.

The gradual rise of Confucianism may be symbolized by the titles given him by Chinese rulers. They were:
1) Duke, AD 1
2) "Foremost Teacher", 637 AD
3) "King", 739 AD
4) "The Perfect Sage", 1013 AD
5) Shang Ti, "Heaven", 1906

Confucianism Under Communism....

In the first half of the twentieth century, religion was in a general state of decline in China. Confucianism suffered because their scholars lost popular respect and temples were largely abandoned.

In 1949, came the victory of Communism in China. To some degree, Confucian morals are still practiced there, but Communists have rigidly opposed ancestor-worship. This is done on a social basis, since this practice could perpetuate clan loyalty above that to Communism.

Is Confucianism a Religion....

Kungfutzu did not repudiate the existence of heaven or spirits. He simply refused to debate or discuss the manner of their existence. He saw religion as an ethical issue, not theological one. What was important to Confucius was not the nature of deity, but the quality of human response to it.

However, Confucius did teach some concepts that could be said to be "theological." He assumed that Heaven stood as the cosmic counterpart to man's ethical responsibilities. He was not opposed to religious rites, but to their performance for selfish purposes. The system which emerged from such premises is a kind of ethical providence. Therefore, a student of Confucius can think of his work and life as being coextensive with the will of Heaven.

By and large, Kungfutzu viewed religious ritual as a factor that contributes to human ethical life. When religion is properly pursued, it offers human disciples moral aspiration and emotional satisfaction. Kungfutzu taught that there is a divine order which works for love and welfare, and he taught that in obedience to that divine order persons will find their highest good.

Confucianism never had a churchly organization, a priesthood, an emphasis on Deity or deities, divinely revealed scriptures or rites of initiation. However, Confucianism may be said to be a religion if religion be defined in terms of social reform and value system creating a life style.

Conclusion....

To the field of world religions, Confucius contributed great ethical teaching, concern for study of the humanities and the basic milieu of the Chinese life style before Communism. Kungfutzu is far from dead and he springs back to life when any person treats another with Li.

BIBLIOGRAPHY

H.G. Creel, *Confucius, the Man and the Myth* (New York: John Day and Co., 1949)

W.E. Soothill, *The Three Religions of China* (Westport, Conn.: Hyperian Press, 1973)

Richard Wilhelm, *Confucius and Confucianism*. (New York: Harcourt, Brace and Jovanivich, 1971)

James R. Ware, *The Sayings of Confucius* (New York: New American Library, 1955)

Chi-Wong:

My name is Chi-Wong and I am an eighteen-year-old resident of Peking. Occasionally my teachers talk about an ancient Chinese teacher named Kungfutzu. I suppose he was bad because he taught a kind of cultural education ideal that was not good for the people. Also, he was in favor of ancestor worship which is bad because our basic purpose now is to build a bright future for China through the people's party. Besides, *The Sayings of Chairman Mao* are most important. He was a great man who had all wisdom and was able to teach it with a thoroughness that Kungfutzu could never have. Once in a while my old grandfather talks quietly about Kungfutzu and Lao-tzu and others he learned of when he was my age. It is too bad my grandfather will die before the revolution is complete here. Then he, too, could see that it is Chairman Mao who was China's greatest teacher.

Mon-Hong:

My name is Mon Hong. I am a seventy-five-year-old tea merchant living in Hong Kong. Sometimes when I open up the store in the morning I see some young boys hanging around in the street corners. Things are not as they were when I was a boy.

Confucius taught us to respect each other as if we were that other person. Respect is something I don't see much of any more. Everyone is running here and there trying to make more money. When I was young, I had to learn to play a musical instrument and to speak of literature and art. Nowadays all my grandsons want is a new bike.

It grieves me that at my funeral there may be no one who will mourn over my passing for three days, as is our custom. Proper etiquette would dictate that those who respect me should do so, but there is so little etiquette among our people anymore. Excuse me, please, there is a customer waiting.

Chapter XII

Taoism

Ancient China had a distinct religion of its own, Featuring belief in all kinds of gods, in the spirits of ancestors, in a supreme power called the "Lord on High," in a type of Heaven and in the existence of an ill-defined soul. That soul consisted of two parts: the heavenly component called the "hun" and the earthly component called the "po." This division definitely reflects the ancient Chinese concept of yin (negative force) and yang (positive force), the interaction of which produces all events and resultant situations.

The ancient Chinese operated on the premise that only the virtuous were favored by Heaven. It was assumed that the most important component of a person's being was his moral character. Heaven had endowed him with a "constant nature" which is basically moral.

Sacrifice, even all ritual, was performed primarily for its ethical significance. Blessing was achieved through moral character, not through magic.

Reflective of these early concepts is the *Book of Odes* a collection of songs sung in religious and official functions during the period from 1000 to 300 BC. Among them are:

Don't you mind your ancestors.
Cultivate your virtue.
Always strive to be in harmony with Heaven's mandate.
Seek for yourselves the many blessings...and

The admirable, amiable prince
Displayed conspicuously his excellent virture
He put his people and his officers in accord
And he received his emolument from Heaven
It protected him, assisted him, and appointed him king.
And Heaven's blessings came again and again.

Depite a prevalent notion in western nations to the contrary, people from the beginning have been as religious as any other people. Ancient China saw the world as filled with spirits. The dead were regarded as an integral part of a social group by both the rulers and the peasants. Shamans were depended upon for spiritual mediation between the living and the dead.

Even the daily routine of cultivating the soil, social etiquette, and political life was regarded as religious and was performed with great fervor. A rich pantheon of spirits, ghosts, and conquered deities formed a court under the supreme deity, "Heavenly Lord," or "Shang Ti."

According to the ancient Chinese, the world of humans and the world of nature constitute a whole governed by reciprocal relationships between the two. Never was a distinction made between the sacred and the secular, only there was one between the ceremonial and informal aspects of religion. Unlike the case in some western religions, the meaning of life was sought in the whole of life and was not confined to any section called specifically "religious."

One ancient Chinese phrased it, "The Chinese are in love with life, with its kings and beggars, robbers and monks, funerals and weddings, childbirths and sicknesses and glowing sunsets and feasting days."

For the ancient Chinese, the world was not created, it simply is. Therefore, the world has no beginning or end and time is a series of ever-repeating seasons. So, "creation" is a constant re-creation of nature and humans are an integral part of nature.

The cosmic eternal order, or Tao, was central to ancient Chinese thought. Changes in the world of nature were not viewed as accidental. Tao, the path which the universe follows naturally, is that force from which all beings evolve.

Tao manifested itself, for the ancient Chinese, in the dual principles of Yin and Yang. The five primary elements of fire, earth, air, wood and metal, for example, are developed out of the alternate actions of Yin and Yang. Although these two forces are opposed in character, they are equally essential for the continuing existence of the universe. So, the fundamental religious concern of the ancient Chinese was to keep the Yin-Yang harmony in tact and to actualize the Tao by not interfering with it.

So, Lao-tze and Kungfutzu (see Chapter XI) did not come to religious vacuum when they proclaimed and demonstrated their truths.

A counterbalance between Taoism and Confucianism in China was also the Realists. The moving force in the Realist movement was Han Fei (280-233 BC), who represented a new breed of government specialist who advocated the power of the state and its expansion.

The Realist school which developed after the third century, BC, rejected all appeals to tradition, all reliance on supernatural sanctions and trust in guidance from above. A fundamental premise to Realism was the rejection of private standards of right and wrong. "Right" came to mean what the rulers in power want and "wrong" means whatever the rulers do not want. Mutual espionage was also a principle of Realist government. The people were organized into groups who were mutually responsible for each other and were obliged to tell higher officials about any crimes against the group committed by an individual. Any member of the group who did not tell was to be punished as if he had committed the crime himself.

The Realists argued that the sole aim of a state is to maintain and expand its frontiers. Food production and military preparations were the only activities which the state was to support. Therefore, the only classes of citizens to be supported by the state were the agricultural laborer and the farmer.

An ancient Realist teacher said "Concentrate the people on warfare and they will be brave. Let them care about other things and they will be cowardly. A people that looks to warfare as a ravening wolf looks at a piece of meat is a people that can be used. In general, fighting is a thing that the people detest. A ruler who can make the people delight in war can become king of kings."

For the Realists, all book learning was seen as inherently evil. So, they taught that the first social class eliminated by the state is the aristocrats, followed by the moralists.

Realism and the primitive animists functioned as the "givens" out of which Taoism was forged.

(A study of the Realists is also important as a background for the present control of China by the Communists.) There are numerous parallels of the two groups, including: emphasis on the military and agriculture, rule by power, distrust of cultural moralists, aversion to philosophers and aversion to merchants who sell "artificially needed" objects.

Original Taoism offered to the animists of ancient China a renewal of religion with emphasis on heaven's unity, nonbeing as the source of Being, nonaction as the way to deliverance and a synthesis between naturalism and mysticism. Therefore, it is ironic that twentieth century Taoism is filled with mysticism, is polytheistic, and has numerous rituals complete with religious paraphanelia. It is evidence of another thin coat of veneer that a new religion may paint over animism. The animism never completely disappears.

Lao-tzu....

The life of the founder of Taoism is clothed in legend. His real name is Li Tan and he was born about 600 BC, fifty years before Confucius. He lived to be about a century old and gave inspiration to most of the *Tao-te Ching* before dying. Beyond that, not much is clear. Legend has it that he was two thousand years old and with a white beard when he was born. Legend also tells of a brief debate with Confucius in which Li Tan, later called Lao-tzu, or "old master" won and rode off on his ox into the mountains. Beyond the fact the "old sage" lived in the sixth century, BC, in ancient China and contributed heavily to the *Tao-te-Ching*, not much is known.

Basic teachings....

Much more can be surmised about Lao-tzu's teachings than his life. The major themes are:

1) The Tao is the principle that underlies nature and all of existence, including society. About Tao, Lao-tzu said:

> The thing that is called Tao is eluding and vague.
> Vague and eluding, there is in it the form.
> Eluding and vague, in it are things.
> Deep and obscure, in it is the essence.
> The essence is very real, in it are evidences.

2) *Wu-wei*. This concept may be defined as "non-involvement" or "in-action." Lao-tzu taught, "Through doing nothing, all things are done. As the inherent principle in nature, Tao operates in the terms of cycles of movements, affecting the harmony of the active and passive

forces of the law of reversal.'' So, wu-wei becomes action according to nature. Asked to comment on wu-wei, Lao-tzu said:

> The world may be known
> Without leaving the house
> The Way may be seen
> Apart from the windows.
> The further you go,
> The less you will know.
> *and*
> So, the Wise Man
> Knows without going
> Sees without seeing
> Does without doing.

3) *Fu*. Lao-tzu taught that an invariable law of nature is the return (Fu) of everything to non-being. The only thing that is permanent is non-being. Each valuable thing, after completing its cycle of existence, returns to nature.

4) *Te*. This concept is ''moral force.''

An old Chinese charcter for *Te* consists of three parts: ''to go,'' ''straight'' and ''the heart.'' Put together, these characters symbolize an inward peace. When one's heart goes straight, his whole being is at peace.

Lao-tzu wrote:

> The sage, putting himself in the background, is always to the fore, remaining outside, he is always there. He does not show himself, therefore he is seen and everywhere. He does not define himself, therefore he is distinct. He does not assert himself, therefore he succeeds. He does not boast of his work, therefore he endures.

The model person, for Lao-tzu, would be one who is at inward peace because he operates with integrity in harmony with nature.

5) *Change*. Lao-tzu observed that when persons begin to look critically at the world and themselves, they find the Tao very much at work. Nothing is stable as change and reversal prevail everywhere. Almost always, what persons consider to be permanent turns out to be changing. See, a true Taoist practices morality in terms of inaction (wu-wei). While he does good deeds, he is not attached to them or anything else which is constantly changing.

6) *On government*. The *Tao-te Ching* contains several chapters on government. In those is found Lao-tzu's primary principle: noninterference by government of the people and vice-versa. Lao-tzu assumed that persons are basically good. Therefore, he warned against the codification and enforcement of moral laws by the ruler. Further, argued Lao-tzu, the ruler should keep the people ignorant. Every person whose knowledge increases naturally increases his desires. He then begins to try to fulfill those desires. Therefore, it is the ruler's duty to keep the people uninformed.

7) *Cosmology*. Lao-tzu taught that, at its crux, the universe is utterly simple and mysterious. It can never be understood completely.

Yet, we remain a part of it as we seek to fathom its meaning. Lao-tzu
The universe is the unity of all things. If one recognizes his
identity with the unity of all things, then the parts of his own
body mean no more to him than so much dirt.

The doctrinal system of Lao-tzu stands in relationship and contrast
to the Realism and animism with which is coexisted. Lao-tzu
prescribed non-involvement so as to realize inner harmony.
Attachment to a changing universe was to him as absurd as seeking
the full meaning of Tao. This stress on flowing with nature stands in
stark contrast to the busy Realists training soldiers and the animists
carving gods. Original Taoism also stands in contrast to serve modern
Chinese still involved in religious ritual in the name of the nonactive,
mystical Lao-tzu.

Is Taoism a Religion....

Taoism, in its ancient form, could be said to be a religion because of
its mythology, including the Tao as the source and order of nature.
Lao-tzu admitted the existence of spiritual beings, but seemed
unconcerned about placating or disturbing them in any manner.
Taoism evolved from a mystical involvement with the Tao into a
full-blown religion in early twentieth century China.

Conclusion....

Though little is known about the life of Lao-tzu, his influence on
Chinese life has been sizable. Flowing with nature is a central motif of
much of the Oriental mindset.

Lao-tzu's establishing of the Tao as an unalterable principle is also
important for subsequent Chinese intellectual development because it
gave rise to science. Lao-tzu stressed the independence of natural
laws. These laws are neutral, devoid of moral attributes and without
regard for what persons may think of them. From their beginning,
Taoists have emphasized the observation of nature. Lao-tzu's
emphases have also served to keep Chinese natural scientists honest
because he stressed the limitations of human reason and a sense of
wonder about the infinite power of nature. Taoism lives on, even in
modern China, wherever an old man sits by a stream knowing that he
and it are ever changing.

BIBLIOGRAPHY

Whittier Bynner, *The Way of Life According to Lao-tzu* (New York: John Day, 1944)

Lawrence G. Thompson, *Chinese Religion: An Introduction* (Los Angeles: Dickenson, 1975)

Arthur Waley, *The Way and Its Power* (London: George Allen and Unwin, 2934)

C.K. Yang, *Religion in Chinese Society* (Berkeley: University of California, 1970)

Fung Yu-Lnn, *A History of Chinese Philosphy* (Princeton, N.J.: Princeton Books, 1952)

Mai-Li:

My name is Mai-Li and I live in Singapore. Ours is a beautiful colony with beautiful trees, mountains and rivers. It is easy to see why my father, who teaches Chinese philosophy at the university, would talk about wu-wei all the time. I have actually seen him cry when he sees pollution in a stream or a tree needlessly injured.

My mother is an artist. In her paintings she highlights rivers and mountains. Sometimes I look a long time before I see any people in them. They are always there. One Englishman who bought her painting said, "In your work, we humans look so insignificant." My mother replied, "Yes, and are we not?"

My brother is a chemist. He lives in the spirit of Lao-tzu, my father reminds him, because he is doing nothing but discovering Tao.

Me, I am unjust Mai-Li. Next year I go to the university to study. I do not know what I will study; however, I am a child of Lao-tzu, the "old sage" who lived long ago.

Wu-Lei:

My name is Wu-Lei. I am a twenty-five-year-old graduate student in political science at a university in Taipei, Taiwan. My master's thesis will be on a comparison between Lao-tzu and Han-Fei on government. Already I can see that they both disagree with Kungfutzu's ideas that everyone should be educated broadly in the humanities.

I especially like Lao-tzu because he believed in a minimum of government. I can see where people do better when left alone. If the politicans are exemplary, the people will operate with grace. However, I must disagree with the "old sage" when he says that the people should be left ignorant. To be informed is important. That is what I am doing in school. I guess Lao-tzu was more than Han-fei, though, because Han-fei taught that education should be mainly to teach people to grow crops and fight. Excuse, me, please the library is opening now....

Chapter XIII

Sokagakkai

There is a religious group which now boast more than sixteen million members in Japan and 225,000 American members in the United States. This group has received little notoriety, even though it has more followers than other "major" world religions as Judaism, Sikhism, Jainism and Zoroastrianism.

Today, this movement, variously called Sokagakkai (Society for the Creation of Value) or Nichiren Shoshu claims among its followers fifteen percent of all college students in Japan. It is also on occasion known by it political arm in Japan, the Komeito, or "Clean Government" party. The Komeito is the third largest political party in Japan, in a multi-party system.

From 1963 to the present, Sokagakkai has averaged winning twenty thousand new converts every month.

The student should note first that Sokagakkai is but one of more than three hundred fifty of the "new religions" in Japan. In 1946, when the United States army and political rulers arrived in post war Japan, a state of martial law was declared and the emperor was forced to deny that he was divine. The state religion of Shinto was officially declared nonexistent. The people of Japan found themselves in a religious identity crisis. Almost overnight the "new religions" sprang up, giving new forms of religious expression to afford the Japanese people a new point of contact with the divine and society. Elements of Shinto reappeared under new forms. No nation makes a complete reversal of religious loyalty in a matter of days, despite political pronouncements to that effect.

All of the "new religions", of which Sokagakkai is a part, have some common elements:

1) Belief in a strong, charismatic person who demands allegiance in an authoritarian fashion, and receives it from loyal sect members.

2) Such shamanistic elements as promises of healing and other physical benefits for being a part of that particular sect.

3) The promise of immediate material benefits are constantly paraded before potential new converts and testimonies of newly acquired monies and other material benefits are given by older members of the movement.

4) The sociological and psychological needs for belonging are reinforced and demonstrated in the "new religions", especially in light of the need for such since the removal of state Shinto as the official Japanese religion in 1946.

5) Youthful vigor is given a channel of release in the "new religions". Large rallies featuring parades of tens of thousands of Japanese youth are common.

6) There is little or no demand for a radical inner change in the "new religions." Repentance and a change in moral life style are simply not on the agenda for the mind set of the new groups in Japan.

7) The "new religions" encourage also a sense of continuity with family and national heritage. Ancient Japanese roots are examined and exploited in a constant attempt to attach "new religious" participants to their national past and ancestral heritage.

Sokagakkai, as a classic example of the "new religions", demonstrates all seven of these elements. In this group, the needed charismatic leadership was supplied by Mr. Josei Toda, the second president of the group. Mr. Toda was so outspoken for Sokagakkai and against state Shinto that he was imprisoned for much of World War II.

The shamanistic elements in Sokagakkai are immediately apparent to the outside observor. Twice daily regular chants to Nam Myoho Renge Kyo (Hail to the Wonderful Law of the Lotus Sutra) are made before the household god sheef containing or displaying the Gohonzon, or sacred scroll. The chant is to be repeated, preferably three thousand times daily. Nichiren chanters frequently spend an hour in the morning and one in the evening on their chants. In return for faithful chanting, Sokagakkai promises physical healing, personal fortune and protection from accidents. Especially worth noting is that the waters at the well at the head temple of Sokagakkai in Japan are purported to possess magical healing powers.

Adherents of Sokagakkai are promised material benefits now! Outside a Sokagakkai temple in Okinawa, there was recently installed a billboard which reads:

"Rewards for Belief: Healing from Sickness, Harmony in the Home, Business Success, Safety on the Sea, Protection from Traffic Accidents."

Testimonies of those participants of Sokagakkai who have received miraculous special material blessings always highlight the meetings and large rallies in the Nichiren Shoshu Association. This is especially true in America.

Mr. Josei Toda taught, for example, that a true believer never goes hungry and that if he is hungry, that is a sure sign that he is not a true believer. So, loyal faith and consistent chanting brings automatic physical watchcare and blessings.

A fourth characteristic which Sokagakkai has in common with other Japanese "new religions" is the reinforcement and solution to the common human need for belonging. The discussion, chanting and testimony meeting, called the Zadankai is the means by which Sokagakkai establishes group identity on the part of its converts. To each of these meetings, the member carries his Shakubuku Kyoten, or "Manual on Forced Conversion." The group leaders are usually non-professionally trained lay persons. The new convert immediately feels himself a vital part of the group, not threatened by some leader who appears to know a lot more than he does. These mass gatherings do much to reinforce the group identity so important to Sokagakkai.

In 1974, more than 100,000 spectators and 14,000 performers jammed the National Stadium in Tokyo. Most of the persons there were under twenty-five years old. This one event is but one among dozens of similar gatherings designed by Sokagakkai leaders to capture and utilize youthful vigor. On these occasions, a hymn is sung which states:

Tho a pistol's pressed against my heart
Not one step back I'd make.
There is only one road for a man to travel —
Eyes up — East — to the dawn!

This stanza makes reference to the ancient Japanese nationalistic symbol of the dawn.

Like the other "new religions" Sokagakkai does not demand a radical inner change through the process of repentance. One Nichiren spokesman says:

The process of salvation is very simple for Sokagakkai. If a man worships a Sacred Object (the Gohonzon) he is saved. If he does not, he is damned. Religious happiness is a key to happiness, which magically opens all doors.

As a final similarity to the other "new religions" one can see in Sokagakkai obvious ties to the Japanese national heritage. Nichiren is presented as the national Buddha, therefore, the great worship object of all people. It is contended by Sokagakkai leaders that no foreign gods are worthy objects of faith for humans, including the original Buddha, who came from India.

So, Sokagakkai has common roots with the other "new religions" in Japan. Worldwide, it claims more followers than any of them.

Brief history....

One Nichiren (1221-1282) was without doubt the most controversial figure in Japanese Buddhism. He was a man of great intensity. It is said by his peers that his brilliant mind would not permit sidetracks. For some, he is described as the Japanese counterpart to the Hebrew prophet Amos, a man of intense drive for social justice.

From the age of twelve, Nichiren devoted himself totally for twenty years to a search for the truth. From the time he was thirty-two years old, he appeared frequently at the military capital, Kamakura, to admonish government officials with his "memorial", or flaming speeches or pantomines on behalf of the common folk.

In 1261, Nichiren went for the first of these, in which he condemned the government officials for not keeping the Buddhist Dharma. As a result, he prophesied a foreign invasion of Japan. The government leaders banished Nichiren to the Izu peninsula for a period of more than two years He was pardoned early in 1264 AD.

The chief religious contribution of Nichiren to Japanese life was his elevation of the Lotus Sutra as the highest of the Sutras in Buddhism. He said that he did this for six reasons:

1) Through knowledge of the Lotus Sutra, all persons can attain Buddhahood.

2) Buddha is eternal, without beginning or end. Therefore, by attaining Buddhahood through knowledge of the Lotus Sutra, one can become a part of *eternal* Buddhahood.

3) The salvation of the original Buddha, Guatama, guarantees the possible salvation of all. Guatama's salvation makes the attainment of Buddhahood a possibility for all who believe in the Lotus Sutra.

4) Guatama made a secret prophecy (now made known through Nichiren) that after his death all his teachings except the Lotus Sutra will lose their power.

5) All bodhisattvas (embodiments of the Buddha ideal) are committed to proclaim the wonderful Lotus Sutra. One can know a false bodhisattva by his failure to elevate the Lotus Sutra.

6) Nichiren will receive untold persuction and hardship in the thirteenth century, AD, but eternal comfort and protection shall be given to all who keep the sacred chant, Nam Myoho Renge Kyo.

The revitalization of modern Nichiren in the form of Sokagakkai owes its beginning to a meeting in 1937 at a Tokyo restaurant. By far the most powerful figure there was Josei Toda (1900-1959), a former elementary school teacher, math scholar and author of textbooks on the subject. It was Toda who gave the new movement a serious drive to win converts. He authored a manual entitled, "The Manual of Forced Conversion." By 1958, he announced that his goal of 750,000 households in Japan practicing Sokagakkai had been reached.

Despite Toda's death in 1959, the figures in 1971 listed more than seven million Japanese households as members of Sokagakkai. The Japanese Sokagakkai Student Department claims a membership of 200,000 in 1978.

In 1965, Sokagakkai began to make serious inroads into the American scene, where it is usually known as the Nichiren Shoshu Association, or NSA. That same year saw the establishment of the American newspaper entitled *The World Tribune*. The newspaper regularly features photos of happy pilgrims who have been to Japan to soak up the miracles of the headwaters at the chief Sokagakkai shrine. Mixed with advertisements aimed largely at Japanese consumers are testimonies of native Americans (non-Japanese) who have found physical and spiritual blessings through chanting. Conscious effort is made through the newspaper to attract non-Japanese Americans.

Because Nichiren Shoshu is growing so rapidly in the United States in the 1970's, an official stance is articulated toward the dominant religion here, Christianity. The official stance is as follows, "In America we were not taking an anti-Christian stance, but a non-Christian one."

Mr. Ikeda, the current world-wide president of Sokagakkai, set out a more militant stance, however, in his inaugural address in 1960:

Sokagakkai is the greatest ally of the people. The enemy
to man is false religion casts men into hell; the upright
Dharma makes of them Buddha. Such is the golden saying of
the great holy one, Nichiren. Taking up his banner, let us his
followers pursue after the extermination of all false religion.

A systematic destruction of all former "idols" held by a new convert have characterized the movement since Ikeda's statements in 1960.

This militance, however, goes back all the way to Nichiren, of the thirteenth century, AD, who said:

The whole world is in rebellion against the right. Men have universally become the slaves of evil. Evil spirits and demons have come to take their places, and calamities and sorrows have befallen us.

While the Shinto Kami, or gods, are rediculed by Nichiren leaders with such statements as, "Praying at a Shinto shrine is like praying to a fishmonger," it is Christianity which is the universal non-Buddhist religion singled out most often for attack. For example, the Christian idea of a personal Creator God is considered to be scientific. Christianity is further frequently characterized as a religion without power to change anyone's present condition. The Christian doctrines of the deity and resurection of Christ are said to be outside rational thought. The contention is that not one of Christ's propheies was fulfilled.

So, here we have modern Sokagakkai in Japan and the NSA in the United States, both owing their origin to a thirteenth century Japanese monk who combined his insistence on the Lotus Sutra as the only way to achieve Buddhahood with a negative view toward "false religions."

Practices....

The most distinctive practice for Sokagakkai is that of Shakubuku, which literally means, "to destroy and conquer." This technique is described and recommended in the sacred book the Nichiren chanters bring to their discussion meetings. The book is the Shakubuku Kyoten, or "Manual on Forced Conversion." This stringent policy of securing new converts makes Billy Graham look like Don Knotts.

It is recommended to Nichiren members as the quickest way to achieve buddhahood in this life, quicker even than chanting to the Lotus Sutra. It is further presented as the quickest way to break the chain of Karma and to reap physical and spiritual merits for oneself.

Tales about Shakubuku include threats to burn down a home in Japan and Japanese students being harrassed, kidnapped, slapped and derived of sleep in America. At any rate, there is no more physically violent manner of achieveing converts in all the world religions.

Worship in Sakagakkai revolves around three activities. First, there is the daily chanting of Nam Myoho Renge Kyo, usually from fifteen to sixty minutes both in the morning and the evening. Second, the weekly public meetings are held. Attendance is expected at these rallies, which include chanting, testimonies and a combination pep talk-testimonial. Third, it is expected that every financially and physically able adult involved in Sokagakkai make at least one pilgrimage to the chief shrine in Japan, wherein is contained a picture of Mr. Josei Toda. Faithfulness to these practices can afford the practitioner such blessings as healings of physical illness, delaying of the day of death for months and even years and the elimination of human misery through the elimination of false belief.

Conclusion....

Sokagakkai is not without its serious critics in Japan, who include one Hirotatsu Fujiwara, who holds a Ph.D. in Political Science from a Tokyo University. He criticizes Sokagakkai for, among other things, its use of political means to spread religious ideas, calling down curses on others, and subtle pressure to deny freedom of speech. (For further details, the student may read Mr. Fujiwara's book listed in the bibliography at the end of this chapter.)

Nonetheless, Sokagakkai is worthy of consideration among world religions for some good reasons:

1) It is a strange wedding of western militarism (Shakubuku) with Oriental mysticism (chanting).

2) It is an amalgamation of politics and religion. On occasion, Sokagakkai has organized six million members to assist Komeito, especially in times of elections.

3) The East/West marriage is illustrated perfectly in its mixture of the material and non-material.

4) Sokagakkai is representative of the prolific and vital "new religions" movement in the past thirty-five years in Japan.

5) Sokagakkai raises the question of the right to and methods of evangelization of other human beings. Its militant stance to other religious traditions is worthy of consideration, if only as a model of sectarianism.

For those who seek further enlightenment, then, it is Eyes Up-East-to the Dawn!

BIBLIOGRAPHY

Noah S. Brannen, *Sokagakkai* (Richmond: John Knox Press, 1968)
Hirotatsu Fujiwara, *I Denounce Soka Gakkai*. (Tokyo: Nisshin Hodo Co., 1970)

Walter:

My name is Walter. I am 39 years old and a resident of California. Lots of people would recognize my whole name if I were to give it. For years I was a professional athlete. Long days and nights on the road drove me apart from my first wife. As divorce came, I discovered a Nichiren Shoshu through a friend. The first time I went to a meeting the noise was deafening as more than two hundred people were chanting loudly. I was turned off.

However, two weeks later I started chanting regularly. It helped me feel better and forget about alimony payments. Soon even my performance on the playing field was helped. My teammates even noticed it.

After my second wife left me I was really depressed. Then I got even further into chanting. Next month I'm going to Japan for the second time. In the meantime, you can bet I'll be chanting and staying eligible for the many benefits of Sokagakkai. Excuse me, please, it is time for my evening chant.

Nakamura:

Hello, my name is Nakamura. I am twenty years old and present of the Student Organization for Sokagakkai on my campus. I-have been a part of the followers of Nichiren all my life as my parents were part of the movement since 1947. Although I never met Mr. Toda personally since he died the year I was born, he must have been quite a man. His superior intellect led him to plan for the student wing of Sokagakkai.

In our local chapter here in Osaka, we do a lot of political campaigning for our party's candidates and a lot of proselyting through Shakubuku. Sometimes the more secular students laugh at us, but most of our peers really respect us for doing what we believe in.

In the summer I'm going to get to work at our shrine. I know I'll meet people from all over the world. Our religion is growing. That's because there are so many benefits to it....

Chapter XIV

The Martial Arts

Grunts and kicks and bows and thrusts fill the air at your friendly neighborhood martial arts studio. This is especially true on Saturdays, known in the trade as "munster days" because of the dozens of American boys and girls eager to learn the latest form of self-defense to impress their peers.

The martial arts craze has been one of the most obvious proofs of the Eastern religions into the United States in the past generation. Black belts abound as the living proof that Americans can and do learn from their oriental instructors the art and philosophy as practiced in the Orient millenia ago.

For more than physical exercise and self-defense techniques, the martial arts are expressive of a way of life dominant in ancient Japan, Korea, India, China and Okinawa. Confusion reigns among the general public regarding the connection between the philosophy and physical in the ancient arts of self-defense. This chapter is presented in the hope of reducing that confusion level.

Basic types....

There are hundreds of schools and subschools of the martial arts, almost as numerous as the schools and instructors within that discipline. However, the major types are as follows:

1) *Judo*

Judo is a predominantly Japanese type of martial art, coming from the two Japanese words, "Ju" and "Do." The two words mean "gentle way." These two words came to signify the mental training that the judo player needs in order to make practical use of the judo philosophy in personal contacts, daily experiences and career relations. The goal of Judo is to teach the maximum efficient use of both mental and physical energy in all areas of life, not just in physical contact. It can be said that judo is an art because it is a method of arriving at self-realization and true self-expression. Judo may also be called a science because it implies mastery of various laws of nature, including gravity, friction, momentum, velocity, weight transmission and unison of forces. The mastery of such forces is used against an attacking enemy as the player "gives way gently" to the opponent's thrust or attack.

Training in judo disciplines the mind through physical, symbolic exercises, also bringing about a mastery of the skill of higher logic. It has the further goal of discovering and developing the true potential within the artist. This can result in the utter serenity of mind.

Japan's history has helped to produce modern judo. In that nation, the martial arts were the sole property of the Samurai class during the feudal (medieval) period. However, by the end of the Tokugawa period (ca. 1867) the Japanese martial arts were systematized and were producing many schools of eminent masters who developed their own styles and techniques.

The late professor Jigoro Kano (d. 1938) learned the jujitsu of the Shin-yo school and devised in 1882 the Kodokaw judo as we have it almost a century later.

The guiding spirit which underlies the old school jujitsu is the morality of bushido. With victory on the battlefield as the original ultimate object, all the daily routine of the warrior's life was regulated and prescribed for this purpose. However, it is against the spirit of the ancient Japanese martial arts to be fond of killing and violence. While having the brave vigor and desire to conquer the enemy, the bushido warrior's mind was broad enough to retain respect for the enemy's life. The technique aims at checking only the opponent's violence and not to destroy his life.

Considered from the "spiritual" side, the Japanese martial arts were from the beginning a form of self-discipline for the perfection of the personality. What was required at the first and last was preparedness for death. If one is ready for death, the judo practitioner is worthy for life.

Thus, when confronted by an enemy, one is awakened to self by facing death. It is then that one comes to view death in the light of life and thereby to regard life and death as one.

This is best summed up in a statement by Dr. Kano:

> There should be one all-pervading principle governing the whole field (of the martial arts) and that principle should be the highest or most efficient use of mental as well as physical energy directed to the accomplishment of a certain definite purpose or aim. Once the real impact of this principle is understood, it may be applied to all phases of life and activity....

2) *Karate*

A second major type of the martial arts is Karate, the title of which comes from a Japanese word meaning "empty hand." The emphasis in Karate is on concentration of as much of the body's power as possible at the point and instant of contact. Striking surface for such concentration include the hands, the ball of the foot, heel, forearm, knee and elbow. Physical toughening is viewed as critical in Karate, but timing tactics and spirit also are seen as vitally important.

Karate evolved in the Orient over a period of centuries. India was the original source of weaponless fighting. Chinese monks learned the rudimentary art from traveling Indian gurus. Karate was systematized in Okinawa in the seventeenth century, AD. It was imported into Japan in the 1920's.

Today Karate is often divided into two types: self-defense and sport. In sport karate, blows and kicks are stopped short, preferebly within an inch of contact. Actual contact is used in the self-defense style.

102

3) *Kung Fu*

A third form of the martial arts is Kung-Fu. It is an ancient Chinese style of karate, probably derived from an even older style of hand and foot fighting which originated in India.

The principal differences between Kung Fu and other styles of karate are a preference for clawing, stabbing hand blows and a different and graceful stylistic manner of practicing the routines, also called Katas, or "forms".

However, it is not correct to think of Kung Fu as if it were one, well-defined style within Karate, for within Kung Fu there are two main divisions and a number of sub-divisions with respect to types of blows preferred, style of practice and general attitude toward the entire discipline.

The two basic styles of Kung Fu are:

1) *Hard style*—
with a clear preference for strength and power techniques, and inclination toward the use of kicks and an emphasis on hand conditioning.

2) *Soft style*—
with emphases on speed rather than power, hand blows rather than foot blows and a preference for vulnerable body targets. This skill of hitting at vulnerable body areas is called the "poison hand."

These are three of the most basic and possible styles within the martial arts. They are particularly popular in the United States.

Relation to Oriental medicine and religions....

Traditional Oriental (particularly Chinese) medicine's weapons against illness are few in number, but are effective. They include the now famous acupuncture and moxibustion (an emerging field in the United States) with therapy achieved by heating instead of needling acupuncture points. Also used in Oriental medicine are remedial massage, herbal remedies and, *most importantly*, exercise. Even today Chinese medical students must take courses in therapeutic exercise throughout their studies. This is in marked contrast to Western medical students, who would never consider such a thing.

The whole Oriental attitude toward the effect of exercises on the body differs radically from those ideas dominant in the West. One goal of Western exercise is bigger and stronger muscles. The Orientals are more concerned with developing stronger internal organs, nerves, joints, ligaments and blood vessels. This is because Oriental medical thought attributes most illness to internal weakness and believes that if weakness is eliminated through exercise there is no room for disease.

For example, in Kung Fu, exercises are done to put one into contact with his inner vital life force. A similar purpose can be found in India's Raja Yoga, whose word for the energizing life force is Atman. Both terms can be translated as "breath", "air", or "energy" and both basically mean that life force that stirs within each of us and makes of each person a living, thinking creature.

In contrast, western medicine sees the human body as a complete and self-regulatory system and believes that the average has few flaws of any seriousness. The Oriental view is that the body is a flawed organism that needs continual regulation to keep it operating efficiently.

Oriental doctors usually ask six questions to assess one's health. They are:

1) Are you free from fatigue?
2) Do you sleep soundly?
3) Is your appetite good?
4) Are you good-humored?
5) Is your memory sound?
6) Are you precise in thought and action?

From the beginning, the martial arts are part of an exercise system that stretches back out of sight into ancient India and China. There has never been a Chinese word "calisthenics" as the western world knows it. The closest would be Kungfu-Wusu, a name for the whole system of developing the body for strength and self-protection.

The Kung Fu man is the folk hero of traditional Chinese culture. He is a cross between a knight in armor and a Wild West gunslinger. He is trained to be as adept in medicine as in self-defense. They are highly trained in the martial arts, but also in the Confucianist tradition, are expected to be "men of letters" and refined in every way. They have to be well versed in Taoist and Confucianist thought and able to write adequate verse and able to play at least one musical instrument.

In fact, it can be said that Taoism and Kung Fu developed along parallel lines. Taoism can be said simply to be a way of achieving higher states of consciousness by following the belief that nature guides all things. (See the chapter on Taoism in this book for further information.) The philosophy of the ancient Kung Fu warrior had its origin in Taoism. Both evolved on the popular level into systems which included breathing, medical, meditation and alchemy techniques.

Kung Fu also has religious roots in Buddhism, particularly Zen. In 530 AD, a Buddhist monk named Ta Mo arrived from India where he had learned Zen and soon set up the Shaolin Temple in Northern China. In a few years, the Shaolin temple became famous for its level of devotion and advancement of Kung Fu through the inclusion of Zen doctrine and discipline.

Popular legend has it that graduation from the Shaolin temple was no simple feat. The potential graduate had to pass three difficult tests before he could leave the temple. As a result, many students stayed as long as ten or fifteen years. They were:

1) A vigorous oral examination on the theory and the history of the art of Kung Fu,
2) Actual combat with a selected number of the better trained monks,
3) A grueling life-or-death voyage through a specially designed sealed maze whose only exit was the front gate of the temple. The maze contained 108 mechanized dummies equipped with wooden fists, razor-sharp spears and knives and a wide assortment of esoteric Chinese weaponry. As the potential graduating student traveled the

length of the maze, some of the boards he walked on triggered the dummies. The dummies were programmed in a random fashion so that the student never knew if he would be attacked by one-three-five at once, or none at all. If the student managed to work his way to the gate, there was one final test.

4) The exit was blocked by a five hundred pound smouldering urn. To gain his freedom, he was required to wrap his arms around the hot urn and lift it out of his way. In the process, the red-hot iron would brand his forearms with two symbols, a dragon on his right arm and a tiger on his left. This marked him as a graduate of the Shaolin Temple, and afterwards he was treated with the utmost honor wherever he went.

As the student sees the connection between the martial arts, medicine and the other dominant forms of religious expressions in the Oriental world, the questions arise, "Do the martial arts constitute a religion?" and "Why include a chapter on the martial arts in a world religions introductory textbook?"

The martial arts do constitute a religion because they contain these elements:

1) A cosmology, or world view, with an emphasis on the continuing conflict between good and evil. This is borrowed from the Yang/Yin formula in ancient Taoism and continues with the motif that one should be prepared to protect himself in a feudalistically violent world. However, until attacked, the purpose of life is to live in harmony with nature.

2) A definite view of the individual based on concepts borrowed from various Oriental religious tradition. The martial arts student learns to be cultured from Confucianism, to be disciplined from Yoga, aesceticism from the Taoist monk and a search for oneness with reality from Zen. So, martial arts participants display a definite, but seldom realized, syncretism of numerous Oriental religions.

Conclusion....

The grunts and black belts and kicks and chops continue on the street corners and basements of America. This is in response to the ancient Oriental call for discipline and defense. Religious assumptions punctuate the grunts, even if unknown to the little kid third from the left on the front row who seems to have difficulty telling his knees from his elbow.

BIBLIOGRAPHY

Bruce, Tegner, *Complete Book of Judo* (N. Y. Bantam, 1967).
Bruce Tegner, *Complete Book of Karate* (N. Y.: Bantam, 1966).
Bruce Tegner, *Kung Fu and Tarchi* (N. Y.: Bantam, 1968).
Michael Minick, The *Kung Fu Exercise Book* (N. Y.: Simon and Shuster, 1974).

Magazine:
"Black Belt", March, 1975.
"Africa Report", July-August, 1977.

Hong:

My name is Hong from Hong Kong. I am twenty-three years old and have been practicing one form or another of the martial arts since I can remember. My life is the martial arts. I hope someday to make monies in America like Bruce Lee. Right now I am third-degree black belt in Kung Fu. My partner and I run a studio for martial arts instruction. We fight in a lot of tournaments and I win most, even though I only weigh 120 pounds.

Kung Fu helps me develop "Chi", that vital energy force residing in me. Because of this, I can face any situation or reason without fear.

Soft-style Kung Fu is my favorite, as I imitate the moves of the dragon, tiger, snake and other animals. It is a beautiful work of art to perfect katas, or "forms" for self-discipline. Ballet-like moves characterize the soft style.

In my nation, martial arts form the favorite sport. We "play" the martial arts for fun. I particularly enjoy watching youngsters learn self-discipline. Perhaps I could give you a lesson when you come to Hong Kong....

Warren:

My name is Warren and I am sixteen years old. I've been the route man. You name it and I've done it! Drugs, sex, crime have all been a part of my scene. I've spent time in three jails and am on probation right now.

Last year I discovered Karate down at the Boys' Club. It's cool, because now my friends know I have a brown belt and have won a couple of tournaments. Now nobody nesses with Warren.

I don't know about this "Chi" and other stuff and neither does my instructor. For me, doing kicks helps me get out my mad. They say it all came from China or somewhere, but I don't care. I've never even been outside the state. Just give me a bag to pound on. Now the guys know I'm the meanest dude on the street.

Chapter XV
Native American Religions

Until recently, almost all writers dealing with the world's religions have omitted the colorful religions indigenous to North America. This omission has led to ignorance about the rituals and beliefs prevalent in that era and area. However, especially in light of the current "Red Power" movement, more Americans are asking about the cultures and religions which are part of the American heritage. In the hope of stimulating further study, this chapter provides a brief study of six great civilizations and their religions. They are the Aztecs, Mayas, Incas, Pueblos, Navajos and the Plains people.

The Aztecs....

Montezuma II ruled the Aztec Empire at its peak early in the sixteenth century, AD, when Hernando Curtez arrived. At that time, a chain of powerful city-states spanned three large lakes in the valley of Anahuac in southern Mexico. Montezuma II was counseled by his astrologers to yield to Cortez although Aztec forces outnumbered the Spainards about twenty to one. This figure indicated the power which the religious leaders have over the emperior. Priests were vested with much power because they supposedly knew the secrets of the gods.

The Aztecs believed that the world would pass through several great ages with overall destruction marking the end of each age. They taught that the age of the 1500's was ruled by a sun god and would end in terrible earthquakes. Their chief god was Huitzilopochtli which roughly translates as "Humming Bird Wizard." He was the god of war and the sun. A powerful goddess was Tonantzin or "Our Mother", whose temple was near present-day Mexico City. Human sacrifice was among the means of asking favor of the gods.

One of the early Spanish explorers told of an Aztec human sacrifice to Huitzilopochtli:

The ascent to the temple was by 114 steps....When we had ascended to the summit, we observed on the platform as we passed, the large stones whereon were placed the victims who were to be sacrificed....Before the altar was a pan of incense with three hearts of human victims which were burning, mixed with copal....With their horrible sounding trumpets, their great knives for sacrifice, their human victims and their blood sprinkled altars, devoted them and their wickedness to God's vengeance, and thought that time would never arrive that I should escape from this scene of human butchery....[1]

---

[1]Charles S. Braden, *The World's Religions* (Nashville: Abingdon Press, 1954).

The Aztec religion was highly developed by the time of Cortez' arrival. A temple was built to an unknown god who was never given a name and never represented in any symbol. An advanced priesthood was accorded with much prestige. Aztec monasteries were established. There was a form of confession. Their ceremonial bathing of the newborn was akin to Catholic infant baptism.

The Aztecs also had a system of penance on personal atoning for sins. These parallels between the Aztec and Catholic systems of faith made it possible for the Catholic priests to adapt very easily and win new converts from the Aztec. For this reason, as much as any other, the Aztec Empire virtually collapsed after the Spanish conquest. A rich heritage of religious faith, although tainted by human sacrifice, was gone except for the memories.

The Mayas....

Mayan culture and religion centered in Central America, primarily in present-day Guatamala. The Mayas were probably the most advanced people of the ancient American world. About six centuries after Christ, the Mayans moved north to Yucatan, where they completely rebuilt their culture.

Most of the Mayan gods were related to agriculture, such as the gods of rain and wind. The lord of the sun was called Kinich Ahau. The god of the underworld was Hon Ahau. As in the case of the Aztecs, the Mayas practiced human sacrifice. The priests were highly revered and ruled over their beautiful temples.

The Mayas had their culture and religion almost totally destroyed by the Spaniards. The Mayan gods, such as Chacs, the god of rain, proved impotent in protecting Mayan culture and religion from the Spanish conquerors.

The Incas....

The Inca Empire which Francisco Pizarro discovered in 1530 stretched from present-day Chile to Columbia. The Incas of the early sixteenth century were a network of peoples stretching back to at least three centuries before Christ.

The chief Incan god was Viracocha, the creator. He carried the title, ''Ancient foundation, lord and instructor of the world.'' All other gods were subject to the chief god, Viracocha. There was also a moon-goddess and a god for each of the chief stars. The Inca heaven was for the faithful, and there was a hell described as very cold with no food.

The Incas separated hundreds of maidens and labeled them ''Brides of the Sun.'' They were guarded and instructed by older women and protected from the world.

The Incan Empire did not succumb to the Spanish invaders as easily as did the Mayan and Aztec Empires. There are still representations of Incan gods to be found among the villages. Incan gods are today far from dead in the village life of South America.

The Pueblos....

The Pueblos are to be identified with the Plateau region of the southwestern United States. The Pueblo civilization can be traced back to at least 800 AD. The main groups are the Hopi, Zuni and Keres. When the Spainards arrived under Coronado, they found about twenty thousand Pueblos with a complex religion based on pleasing the gods of agriculture.

The main god of the Hopis is Masawu, the god of death. The Hopis believe that they are born by emerging from the underground world near their village. After death they simply return to the underworld through an entrance within walking distance from their own village. Masawu, as the god of death, is sometimes referred to as "Skeleton Man." If he is ever met face to face by a Hopi, this is a sure sign of death.

Masawu lives in the underworld and many Hopis see parallels between him and the Christian idea of Satan. He is often described by the Hopis as "the god of the fire." As "god of the fire," Masawu's dwelling place is described in vivid terms.

The Zunis, like most Pueblo Indians, thought that the dead returned to the underworld and became the source of all crops. Therefore, the Zunis prayed to the dead for rain.

For the Keres, the highest god is "Thinking Woman" who is creator and is supreme among the gods. She is also called the "Great Mother." She may incarnate herself as the "Corn Mother" to aid in the growing of grain. These deities are supposed to protect the Keres from danger also.

The Navajos....

The Navajos currently live on the largest reservation in the United States, including parts of Arizona, New Mexico and Utah. The Navajos arrived in what is now New Mexico about 1000 AD. They became close to the agriculturally minded Pueblos and began to settle from their former life as nomads. During the seventeenth century, livestock became a part of their life. During the 1860's, the Navajos were forced to sign a treaty placing them on a small reservation. The current population is more than 100,000 Navajos on a reservation of some 24,000 square miles. Many Navajos live in such metropolitan areas as Chicago.

The creation myth of the Navajos describes four underworlds which have emerged to produce the fifth and present world form. In the first world, called the Black World, man was formed from the meeting of two clouds. Meanwhile, the first woman was formed on the opposite side of the first world. Then the first man came over to live with her. When the first world became overcrowded with coyotes, ants, spiders and bats, the first man and first woman moved up to the second world. After fighting with birds, the inhabitants of the second world went up to the third world. They found the third world to be inhabited by Holy Beings. The fourth world they deserted for the present fifth world.

Navajos do not have one Supreme Being but instead worship many gods. Native Navajo religion places great emphasis on the sun which helps to correlate the universe.

The songs, prayers and hymns of the Navajo Ritual are majestic. A song frequently sung by medicine men is:

Now I walk with Talking God.
It is with his feet I go;...
With goodness and beauty *before* me I go;
With goodness and beauty *behind* me I go;
With goodness and beauty *above* me I go;
With goodness and beauty *below* me I go;
With goodness and beauty in all things around me I go;
With goodness and beauty I follow immortality.
Thus being I, I go.[2]

The Plains people....

The Plains Indians were called Cheyenne, Crow and Sioux by the whitemen, but they called themselves simply "The People." Their religion centered around the Medicine Wheel, which afforded for them an understanding of the universe.

One begins with his understanding of the Medicine Wheel by relating it to his immediate human family and friends. Then he relates himself to the world of the animals, trees, grasses and all other living things.

Any object or abstract idea may be placed at the center of the Medicine Wheel. A mountaintop or a person may be at the center of it. Each person is viewed as the center of a medicine wheel who came to earth to understand and experience limitation. All beings are born lonely and this is relieved by touching. In this way of touching, facilitated by mutual involvement in the Medicine Wheel does one become a Total Being.

Further, according to "the People," each person has a particular animal reflection, direction, color and quality of personality. For example, if a person is born with the mark of the Mouse, he would have the quality of seeing things close up with insight. If a Mouse Person were born in the north, he would have the gift of the mind, so he would be a person intellectually gifted and with unusual capacity for insight. If his color were green, he would be born with an innate capacity for innocence and trust.

After learning of his birth, each person is to develop his life by learning from each of the other directions. If a Mouse Person stayed in the north, for instance, he might be a cold intellectual with no capacity for feeling. The purpose of learning from other beings and powers is to be a balanced person in every aspect of the personality.

Man is particularly important to the Medicine Wheel because only persons are 'determiners.' In one's touching other humans, he learns of wholeness.

Each person carried a shield of one kind or another. They were interpreted by the white soldiers to be providing protection in battle, but this was never the purpose of the shield. The symbols on the

---

[2]"Song of Talking God," *The Navajo Yearbook* (Window Rock, Arizona: Navajo Agency, 1961), p. 523

shield told who the man was, what he hoped to be and what his loves and fears were. Each shield was designed by elders among "the People" after the Vision Quest, a teenage or puberty initiation rite into manhood. The shields were carried by the men so that everyone in the tribe would know them. Their shields were placed outside the lodges when they rested so that the visitor would know the nature of the man inside. The women made their medicine signs visible by symbolic designs woven with porcupine quills.

The following incident conveys part of the struggle to remain "Indian" in the modern American culture by use of the Medicine Wheel.

"The name of the story is Snow White," Green Fire Mouse answered, as he sat up and began his story. "You see, once upon a time...." "What was the symbol of the mirror in the story, Grandpaw?" Rocky asked as they fished.

"It is the people. It is the circle, and it is the shield," answered Green Fire Mouse. "But it is more than that. It is also the law."

"Are there more teachings, Grandpaw?" Rocky asked.

"Sure," the voice again answered from under the hat. "There is the entire world and everything in it that can teach you much, much more. There are the songs, the bibles, the cities, and the dreams. Everything upon the earth and in the heavens is a mirror for the people. It is a total gift. Jump up! And you will see the Medicine Wheel."[3]

Current Movements....

Two current religious movements are greatly affecting the native American. They are "peyote" and "Red Power."

Officially known as the Native American Church, the movement called "peyotism" mixes the use of the peyote node with the experience of "medicine power." Advocates of the use of "peyote" claim it is consciousness expanding. Peyote is a small, carrot shaped cactus which grows in the Rio Grande Valley and southward into Mexico. It contains nine narcotic alkaloids which produce psychedelic effects when taken. Peyote has been used by American Indian tribes for centuries but only recently has become a part of an organized cult. Peyote is said by Mescalero Apache devotees to be useful in finding lost objects and in foretelling the future as well as for healing. Each participant in a ceremony usually takes about four nodes or drinks tea made from the plant.

Healing in peyote meetings is of prime importance and in many cases is the main purpose in calling a meeting. Preaching, stressing injunctions against extramarital sex and the use of alcohol and tabacco is employed as well.

---

[3]Hyemeyohsts, Storm, *Seven Arrows* (New York: Harper and Row, 1972) p. 371

111

Quanah Parker, the great Camanche spreader of the use of peyote was cured of a stomach ailment in 1884 and became an effective proponent of the herb in the late nineteenth century.

John Wilson, the chief "prophet" in the early stages of the Native American Church, appeared first in the Ghost Dance Movement of the 1890's. He was one-half Delaware, one fourth Caddo and one fourth French. At about age forty, he went from the quiet life of a Caddo Indian in Oklahoma to spreading the use of peyote. John Wilson was influenced by Roman Catholic teachings and felt compelled to relate peyotism to Christianity. He argued that the white man was guilty of the crucifixion of Christ. The native American, on the other hand, was innocent of the blood of Jesus. He was to receive his direction from the Peyote spirit, whereas Christ was sent on mission to the white man.

Early in 1976, this author attended a peyote weekend meeting in Oklahoma. About two hundred gathered from various tribes. The women and children stayed outside the circular enclosure with one entry door. The men would emerge on occasion to get some fresh air, appearing a bit giddier each time. The meeting ran from about sundown on Friday until almost sundown on Sunday.

One young girl was brought to be healed and was pronounced healed from a crippled leg on Saturday evening. There was little antogonism to the presence of a white man there. It was obviously a time of celebration and ceremony with an emphasis on community and healing.

The "Red Power" movement is greatly influencing the modern native American in the rediscovery of his rich cultural and religious heritage. The National Indian Youth Council was formed in August of 1960 to help preserve the Indian heritage. Many among the Indian youth are responding to such words as these by a Chickasha, Kenneth Kale:

> We all know about
> Our redskinned counterpart
> Of Martin, Gregory and Stakeley
> Rolled into one —
> Like an angry "Red Muslim"
> With work to be done....
> I've often wondered why it is said
> That the Indian Spirit is broken and dead
> When in their midst like a grizzly bear
> Is the sleeping redskinned giant
> Nor on the prowl.[4]

The modern native American struggles for identity in a white world. A recent study of the Sioux exhibits this plight:

> The Sioux of today live between two worlds without being completely at home in either....He picks and chooses from

---

[4]Stan Steiner, *The New Indians* (New York: Harper and Row, 1968), p. 46

each system what is most expedient at the moment....At the present time, except for a few elderly people, all Indians in these reservations consider themselves as belonging to a Christian denomination, but still believe in the supernatural power of Shamans and resort to them when modern medicine fails them.[5]

In reaction to this, "Red Power" advocates strive to give native Americans identity by helping them to see differences between their cultural values and those of the white man. For example, it is frequently noted that Indians seem unable to externalize themselves in terms of building up material goods. This is because, at native American roots, there is no worry or concern for the future. Traditionally, the land had plenty for everyone. Piling up great possessions implied a mistrust of the Great Spirit.

Further there is a rediscovery of the native American emphasis on all of creation being interwoven when Young Chief, a Cayuse, refused to sign the Treaty of Walla Walla, he said it was because he felt that the rest of creation was not involved in the agreement. He asked, "I wonder if the ground has anything to say?"

The native American often exhibits a lack of any fear of death. Young Chief Joseph, the famous Nez Peace leader, remained at inner peace when his valley was invaded by whites. He told his son as he was dying:

My son, my body is returning to mother earth and my spirit is going away very soon to see the Great Spirit Chief. My son, never forget my dying words. This land holds your father's body. Never sell the bones of your father and your mother.

Here can be seen the fundamental concept of life as a continuing unity involving land and people. Almost universally the native American lives unafraid of death. The "Red Power" movement is being successful in rekindling the native American's pride in such ancient reassurances.

Conclusion....

The ancient American religions deserve attention for this richness of heritage and emphasis on such valuable insights as the identification of all nature to each of its components. The native American weeps when he looks at his land but not at his heritage.

---

[5]E.E. Hagen and Louis C. Shaw, *The Sioux on the Reservations* (Cambridge Institute of Technology) pp. 15-16.

BIBLIOGRAPHY

Storm Hyemeyohsts, *Seven Arrows* (Harper and Row, 1972).

Stan Steiner, *The New Indians* (New York: Harper and Row, 1968).

Ruth M. Underhill, *Red Man's Religion* (Chicago: The University of Chicago Press, 1965).

Red Eagle:
My name is Red Eagle, or Wilbur Robertson. I am a businessman in Tuscon where I run a store featuring turquoise and silver jewelry. I am forty years old and have one son who has just started college.

All the people in my tribe call me Red Eagle. In the white man's business world, I don't use that name much. It hinders me.

Now, do not misunderstand me. I am proud of my heritage and sometimes I even go to our dances where I put on feathers and the whole bit. About two generations ago, most of my family became Mormon. That is the church I go to. But, sometimes after services, particularly on Monday night, I go down to the basement and beat my old grandfather's drum. Then I feel good. I feel Indian.

White Feather:
My name is White Feather and I am a seventeen-year-old female resident of New Mexico. We live in a hogan fifty miles from the nearest store. At times it gets lonely here, but our family knows that we must tend our sheep as we have done for generations past.

My father got involved in the "Red Muslim" movement about the time I was born. He has little use for the white man and his ways. So, we live as far away from them as we can.

At night we talk about our Hopi heritage. My father tells me that I should be proud to be Hopi for we are part of a mighty people. Sometimes I wonder where our might has gone. Perhaps I will learn when I go to college in Sante Fe. In the meantime, I am glad to be Hopi.

Chapter XVI
Communism As Religion

Remember the numbers 10 and 8 and 6 and 3. In today's world there are 10 hundred million (one billion) persons living in lands ruled by Communism. There are 800,000,000 Christians, 600,000,000 Moslems and 300,000,000 Buddhist. So, there are almost as many Communist-influenced persons today as there are Christians and Buddhists combined.

Is Communism a religion? Does Communism deserve a chapter in a book on world religions? The answer is in the affirmative. While classic Communism denies the existence of God, so does classic Buddhism. Further, Communism has at least these trappings of a religion:

1) A founder, Karl Marx
2) An eschatology, i.e., a view of the future
3) A value System
4) An ethic

It will be shown in this chapter that Communism has every right to be labeled a religion. It forms the reference point for developing life styles among persons more than any other ideology in the modern world.

Background....

Communism is a term which implies a common interest and mutual sharing of that which is possessed in common.

This concept is found in Plato's *Republic*. In that work he presented a picture of an ideal state. He urged the abolition of private property among the upper classes.

A second source of early Communist thought was the church. The church of the first century, as described in *Acts*, was characterized by a communal life, the sharing of material wealth and the caring of the poor by the rich. These were integral parts of the first century church.

In 1516, Sir Thomas More published his *Utopia*, in which he called for the abolition of private property in English society. He urged also the development of communal living.

It was William Frederick Hegel (1770-1831) who was most influential in the formation of Marxist thought. He majored in philosophy and theology at the University of Tubingen, where at the age of twenty, he received the degree of Doctor of Philosophy. As he grew older, Hegel contributed these basic ideas to the philosophy of early nineteenth century Europe:

1) Unity of being, i.e., individual parts are not merely differing modes of the Absolute. Rather, they represent stages in the rational development of life. The universe represents a coherent whole.

2) The real is rational and the rational is real. Reason governs all aspects of life and is the key to reality.

3) To discover truth logically, one begins with a thesis standing for affirmation. This thesis is joined by a antithesis standing for the negative. The two are united in a synthesis. A simple illustration of this would be red as the thesis, blue as the antithesis and purple as the synthesis.

4) Conscience is not autonomous. We must look to social institutions for aid in our moral striving.

5) The state is the supreme human institution because in it is found expressed the ideal of reason. This helped give the death blow to eighteenth century individualism.

It was Hegel who laid the groundwork for Marx in that he came up with the thesis-antithesis-synthesis method of discovering truth. Marx could build on this dialectical (paradoxical) method to popularize his theories of economics and politics.

Hegel was followed by Ludwig Feuerbach (1804-1872), who asserted that our religious life depends on our wishes. Religion, he argued, is simply the projection of our own human qualities on the supernatural. Feuerbach severely criticized the Christianity of his day, saying that it had come to represent a religion of complacency. The most remembered phrase which Feuerbach wrote was, ''Man is what he eats.'' By this he meant that our physiological processes influence our thinking. It was Feuerbach who lent Marx a critical attitude toward organized religion as he challenged the shallow, wish-fulfillment oriented Christianity of his day.

Karl Marx....

The stage was now set for the career of Karl Marx (1801-1883). His father was a Jewish lawyer converted to the Christian faith when young Karl was but six.

As a student, Karl Marx was interested in becoming a professor. When he failed to obtain a job teaching, he got a job as a reporter on a radical newspaper in Cologue. In 1845, Marx moved to Paris where he became editor of the *Franco-German Yearbook*. It was there he met Frederick Engels.

Marx moved to London in the late 1840's, where he experienced extreme proverty with his new bride. In 1848, he wrote the *Communist Manifesto* and in 1867 *Das Kapital*, which has become the ''Bible'' of modern Communism.

It is evident in all of Marx's writings that he was influenced by Hegel, Feuerbach, and Engels, among others. From Hegel he observed that history is not a static product, but is full of movement toward a more ideal synthesis. From Feuerbach he borrowed the concept that all the gods of history have been culturally conditioned.

Marx attacked Christianity on two counts:

1) The only reality is matter in motion. Therefore there is no Beyond.

116

2) Christianity supports the affluent way of life. It has given support to the *status quo* for the masses who are taught to remain content in their poverty so they can be rewarded in heaven much later.

As a result of these critical statements, Marx postulated a system only interested in the present. Only by abandoning religion with its other worldly hopes can persons be really happy.

When Marx wrote about history, he pictured it as consisting of a constant class struggle. But, this struggle will end when a classless society is produced when the powerless are liberated. This he based on his call for economic change, believing that a political utopia will result when economic revolution comes.

Karl Marx did not operate out of a political, religious or philosophical vacuum when he wrote the papers which were to influence the world as no others in the next century and a half. His Jewish, Christian, Hegelian and Feuerbachian roots shine through in all his premises.

Nicolai Lenin....

Lenin was born in 1870 to a middle class family who were faithful to the Russian czar at first. His eldest brother, however, was hanged for being part of an attempt to murder Czar Alexander III. Nicolai was expelled from the University of Kogan for revolutionary political activity. He was a student of Karl Marx's writings and was arrested in 1895 and sent to Siberia for three years of exile. In 1900, he left Russia. In 1917, he returned to begin the "October" Revolution.

Lenin was a superb organizer and activist. He brought Marxist thought to bear on the specific situation of Russia in the early twentieth century. For Marx, the liberation of the working class from the capitalists is the task of the working class itself. For Lenin, it was different. He called for a class of middle class intellectuals who could inspire the working masses with a spark of revolution. Lenin argued for a temporary rule of the intelligensia to wipe out the last vestiges of exploitation by the rich capitalists.

Lenin died in 1924. It was he who had helped Marx's "inevitable" theories to come to fruition.

Basic ideas....

Modern Communism is based on key ideas. The Communist perception of reality is along these lines:

1) Communism is an international movement. It follows, therefore, that national loyalties must be subjected to loyalties toward the working classes.

2) The state, in any form, will one day become unnecessary and die away. (Critics of Communism wonder out loud when this will come since it has been more than sixty years since Lenin's revolution.)

3) The economic ideal is "from each according to his ability, to each according to his needs." In that ideal society, produced by Communism, the healthy workers will so produce as to care adequately for the elderly and handicapped.

4) The goal is a "Classless" society. There will be a few inevitable

differences in individual abilities, but no large classes of rulers and the ruled will be in existence in the Communist ideal life.

5) Every segment of economic activity must be publicly owned and operated. Profits are inherently evil and only tend to allow a few to amass wealth at the expense of the masses.

6) The successful revolution must be followed temporarily by the establishment of a dictatorship to start the new society. This will be only temporarily necessary for such matters as stifling anti-revolutionary activities.

7) Capitalism has within it the seeds of its own destruction. Given adequate time, it will crumble from within. This will happen because the gap between the wealthy and the poor will widen. The poor will become more frustrated and revolt.

8) Class conflict is inevitable as long as different classes exist in a society. This is because the capitalist class uses the state to maintain its dominant position at the expense of the poor.

9) Economic motives and processes are always dominant. The basic economic outlook of a society will determine its political and social characteristics. It is economics which rule every other aspect of a society.

10) Human history is in a constant state of flux. History is the story of forces which generate contrary forces. These two interact so that a third force results. So, any social movement such as capitalism necessarily creates an opposed movement such as the poor. The result is a new movement such as Communism. This thesis-antithesis -synthesis view of history is borrowed directly from Hegel.

11) The temporary Communist Party must consist of a hard core of professional revolutionists. The poor will have to be inspired and motivated from outside their own ranks.

12) The true value of any commodity should be measured by the amount of labor used to produce it. However, capitalism operates toward its own downfall by the use of "surplus value." It is from this "surplus value" that the affluent classes grow at the expense of the poor masses.

These tenets of Marxist thought are basic. They may occasionally shift in emphasis as applied to specific situations, but they provide the framework for Communism as a system.

In China....
The Chinese Communist Party was formed in Shanghai in 1921. The years 1945-49 are designated by Chinese Communist historians as the "Third Revolutionary Civil War." In 1949, Chiang Kai-shek and his nationalist forces were driven to Taiwan. On October 1, the Communist leaders proclaimed the existence of the "People's Republic of China."

Today Chinese Communism is a unique entity, with certain characteristics of its own. They include:

1) Resort to Guerilla warfare in the 1950's.

2) Large dependence on the training of the peasant masses.

3) Any deviance among the masses from socialist theory is treated as the works of treason.

4) Mao was pictured as the wise father in the Taoist-Confucianist tradition

5) Communism is used to serve Chinese nationalism

6) "People's communes" in which up to five thousand families were joined together for production

7) Spasmatic "cultural revolutions" in which those who differ radically from Chinese Communist leadership are eliminated.

As one might guess, Chinese Communism has twisted original Marxian to suit its own purposes. This has given to the Chinese experiment its distinct flavor.

In the United States....

The Communist Party, USA, was officially established in 1919. In 1921, the Worker's Party of America was formed to serve as a legal outlet for American Communist activities. Candidates were nominated for President and Vice-President of the United States in 1924.

The CPUSA has tried various tactics to increase the popularity of Communism in America. The most successful has been the formation of a "united front" between Communists and other groups. This has proven moderately successful during the depression of the 1930's and the USA-USSR coalition of World War II.

All in all, Communism has not made much impact on American society from an open attack.

A call for dialogue....

Intense dialogue has been taking place since the early 1960's in Europe and Latin America. The results have been phenomenal on both sides of the conversation. Communists have admitted the naivete of their view of man; i.e., that he is able to lift himself out of his own squalor by the use of man-made forces and techniques. Christians have been forced to produce an ethic including an end time on this earth characterized by justice. It has dawned on Christian participants in those dialogues that any set of ideas bound to the justification of established ruling class makes dialogue and Christianity impossible. Christianity is correctly being seen in the light of the realization that it cannot be concerned exclusively with the private faith of the individual, but in the building of a justice-oriented society.

These Christian-Communist dialogues have produced outstanding Christian spokesmen for a theology of hope. One of these is Jurgen Moltman, of the University of Tubingen. Dr. Moltman, criticizes Communism's perversions as lying in the expectation that the expected "human emancipation of man will come automatically when the economic liberation of men in the socialist industrial state has taken place."[1]

---

[1] Thomas W. Ogletree (editor) *Openings for Marxist-Christian Dialogue* (Nashville: Abingdon Press, 1969), p. 98.

This successful dialogue is proof that Communists and Christians can converse and even change. When representatives of peoples numbering almost two billion converse, the world listens.

Conclusion....

Modern Communism operates on premises about human beings, society, God and the future. It supplies a billion people with a value system. Communism qualifies as a religion for it is a system to which persons give ultimate allegiance. Its future will be determined partly by its ability to coexist with Christianity and other major religious systems of our day.

BIBLIOGRAPHY

Emile B. Ader, *Communism: Classic and Contemporary* (Woodbury, New York: Barron's Educational Series, Inc., 1970)

Herbert Aptheker, *The Urgency of Marxist-Christian Dialogue* (New York: Harper and Row, 1970)

Roger Garandy, From *Anathema to Dialogue* (London: Collins, 1967)

Roger Garandy, *Marxism in the Twentieth Century* (London: Collins, 1970)

Gustane Wetter, *Dialectical Materialism* (New York: Frederick A. Praeger, 1960)

Seng-Chao:

My name is Seng-Chao. I was born in 1949 when the People's Republic of China was created. Life for me in Peking is good. My wife, three children and I live in a two-bedroom house. Everyday I go to work at the auto assembly plant. We are very proud of our work there. My wife attends meetings for studying the sayings of Mao one day a week. At the factory, we take a half hour each morning to do exercises and a half hour in the afternoons to study the little red book.

My favorite times are when I can take my family to a volleyball match or to a large rally in the stadium. It is impressive to see my children participating in marches to show our solidarity as a nation. We do, after all, live and eat better than my father did at my age. Communism has given a dignity back to our people.

Guillermo:

My name is Guillermo. I am a university student in Rome and a member of the Communist Party. We expect to win the big elections here in 1980. The people of Italy are so poor, we believe that Communism has got to be an improvement.

I grew up in the Catholic church. There I learned that God calls persons to give and work for the sake of others. Maybe that is why I am so sure of that now.

At the university I read Marx, Lenin and Mao. From them I learned that the poor must be led in revolt against the rich. I also learned that a few informed ones at the top must do the leading. That is what our party is doing.

The other day I saw my old parish priest. He wanted to know why I had left religion. I told him I have found a religion, one that helps people live better *now*.

Chapter XVII
The Parsis

Currently in Iran, the land where Zoroastrianism was founded, there are fewer than twenty thousand followers of this religion. However, in India there are more than one hundred-fifty thousand Parsis (the name given to adherents of Zoroastrianism). Thus, the Parsis have the distinction of belonging to the world's smallest religion classified as major. There are far fewer Parsis, for example, than Christian Scientists in the world. Yet, Zoroastrianism has had a major influence on the other three major forms of monotheism: Islam, Judaism and Christianity. For this reason alone, the Parsis are worthy of study.

Brief history....

The land of Persia in the centuries before Christ was one of almost barren desert where life itself was a struggle for existence against the elements. The religion of that day was a form of nature worship in which such elements as the sky and the rain were worshiped as powers. Fire was given special reverence and is still used in worship by most modern Parsis.

The major literary sources that deal with this period are the *Gathas* or hymns of early Zoroastrianism. They present the pre-Zoroastrian world as composed of many gods and the resultant human world as being fragmented. The overall picture that emerges is desert animism, with appeasement made to many gods toward the desired end of simple survival.

The people were Aryans or "noble ones". They worshiped a series of gods, known generally as daevas and connected with the basic elements of fire, earth, water, the sun and the moon. One god who had more power than most was Mithras, viewed as the god of light. Zoroaster attempted to elevate Ahura Mazda above all other of these gods, but Mithras would not be completely displaced and emerged later as a chief consort to Ahura Mazda. When Roman soldiers heard of Mithras, they saw him as giver and protector of life. A Mithras cult gained popularity about the time of Christ and some believe that Mithraic worship practices had a direct effect on early Christianity. (Not so incidentally, the birthday of Mithras was celebrated on December 25.)

The argument about the date of the life of Zoroaster, also called Zarathrustra, is one of long duration. Estimates of the time when he lived range from 1500 BC to 400 BC. However, the generally agreed upon date is the seventh century, BC, or contemporary with the original Buddha in India and Jeremiah in Israel.

The *Gathas*, seventeen chapters in the holy writings of Zoroastrianism, form the major source of Zoroaster's life. According to them, he was born of a warrior clan and lived a quiet life until age fifteen, when he put on the Kusti, or sacred string belt symbolic of his entry into manhood.

Zoroaster lived with his parents until about age twenty when he left home to begin a religious life. At about age thirty, he received a divine call from Ahura Mazda to be a teacher and spiritual protector of his people. Zoroaster prayed and gave himself as a living sacrifice to his god. For ten years he preached without a convert, until his cousin was persuaded. Two years later, at age forty-two, Zoraster was able to convert a powerful chieftain by the name of Kavi Vishtaspa. The next thirty years were spent in holy wars spreading the faith. The circumstances of the prophet's death are not recorded in the *Gathas*. Legend has it that an enemy soldier found the seventy-seven year-old prophet tending the sacred flame in the fire temple in Zoroaster's home town of Turan and killed him.

Cyrus ruled Persia from 588-530 BC and probably had been influenced by Zoroaster, who died about 570 BC. The Jews came under Persian control in 538 BC, when Cyrus conquered Babylon. The post-exilec Jewish community reflected ideas and names not common in pre-exilic Jewish thought. For example, Old Testament literature written after the Babyloian and Persian exile mention the name "Satan" four times, although there is no mention of him in pre-exlic writings. Other themes are also added to Jewish theology as a result of contact with the Persians, including:

1) The resurrection of the body;
2) Life after death divided between heaven and hell,
3) God's plan to bring the earth to an end;
4) A day of judgment;
5) Angels and demons.

Concerning Cyrus, one scholar says:

> Cyrus the Great was a Zoroastrian but not a very strict one,...But Darius I and Xerxes after him did no such compromising; they uniformly honored Ahura Mazda, in their many inscriptions, as supreme Lord of Heaven and Earth. Their religion was not any longer precisely that of Zoroaster, as presented in the *Gathas*; but they believed firmly that Ahura Mazda and the agencies of his divine working and favor were with them. [1]

Many scholars think that the Jews got the idea of the devil directly from the Zoroastrians under Cyrus. Among those is Charles F. Potter, who wrote:

> A careful Bible student with any historical sense is forced to recognize how very plainly the fact stands out that the Hebrews borrowed the devil from the Zoroastrians....Before the Captivity, they had no devil in their theology....The theology of post-exilic Judiasm had a devil. Since the Zoroastrian religion of that time strongly emphasized a chief

---

[1] John B. Noss, *Man's Religions* (New York: The MacMillan Co., 1963), p. 478.

among evil spirits called 'The Adversary' and since the post-exilic Jews called their devil 'Satan', which means 'The Adversary', there can be only one possible inference. [2]

As evidence, the story of King David's numbering of the Hebrews is compared in the two records: pre-exilic II Samuel 24 and the post-exilic I Chronicles 21. Note the difference:

| II Samuel 24:1 (Berkeley) But the Lord's anger was inflamed against Israel, and one aroused David against them saying, Go: number Israel and Judah. | I Chronicles 21:1 (Berkeley) Satan, however, stood up again-st Israel and aroused David to take a census of Israel. |

Christianity is heir to these concepts, as well, as Hebrew thought reflected Persian Zoroastrian during the time of Jesus of Nazareth.

When Persia fell to Greece under Alexander the Great in the fourth century, BC, the heighth of Zoroastrianism fell with it.

There was a brief revival of Zoroastrianism in the third century, AD, under the Sassanid rulers in Persia.

In 651 AD, the Moslems invaded Persia. They treated the Parsis as slaves, regardless of the fact that both religions view God as one. The persecution was so intense that Parsis began to flee to India in great numbers about 700 AD. They were welcomed in India and began to grow. On occasion, the Parsis have assisted the Hindus in fighting the Moslems. Recent years have seen the Parsis dwindling in numbers and settling around Bombay in their adopted land of India. The Zoroastrians in Iran today are known as "Babara", or "infidels" by the Moslem majority.

Basic teachings....

Zoroaster contended that his teachings were from God and are universally applicable to every person. He further stressed that every person should exercise his free will in choosing for or against religiousdoctrines.

God.-Zoroaster elevated Ahura Mazda to be the one supreme God. He proclaimed Ahura Mazda as the creator and sustainer of the universe. The name Ahura means "lord". Mazda means "all wisdom". The two words combined mean "all-wise lord."

Even though Zoroaster presented Ahura Mazda as ruling above and supreme, there are in the heavenly host six "Ahuras" or divine attributes. The first three are masculine and the last three are feminine. They are:

1. Asha - knowledge of the law of God and the resultant righteousness, truth and order.

2. Vahu Manah - love, proper mind, thought and disposition.

3. Kshathra - power, dominion, mixed with loving service.

4. Aramita - piety and love.

5. Haurvatat- prosperity, welfare, health, wholeness and perfection.

6. Ameretat-immortality and eternal life.

Faithful Parsis pray daily that these six attributes may be a part of their home.

---

[2]Archie J. Bahm, *The World's Living Religions* (New York: Dell Publishing Co., 19640 1964), p. 249.

Good and evil....

For Zoroaster, a good god and a lying devil are constantly marring against each other. There is no neutral ground. Life is a struggle between good and evil. Ahura Mazda is for the good and has as his helper Mithras or "Light." The Lie Demon, representative of the evil force, was called Ahriman. Zoroastrianism was the first religion to have a fully developed scheme of demonism. A frequently mentioned one was Aeshma the demon of wrath, who stalks the earth, polluting it and spreading disease and death.

Man....

For Zoroaster, persons are constantly in the process of choosing. They are born in a sinless state and can choose to serve either good or evil, Ahura Mazda or Ahriman. All persons will be judged on the basis of their fight against evil. So, life consists in a struggle to find the good. Persons are perfectly free to decide on a continuing basis for good or evil and thus are to be held accountable for their choices. This is clear in the following quote from Zoroaster:

> Before you choose which of Two Paths to tread
> Deciding man for man, each one for each;
> Before the great New Age is ushered in
> Wake up, alert to spread Ahura's word.[3]

Last things....

For the Parsis, each person will receive his just reward at the end of life. The judgment will be based simply on whether a particular person has done more good than evil.

At death, the inner core of a person stays with the body for three days and meditates upon the deeds that were done in life. On the fourth day, he passes to the place of judgment. The inner core, or soul, of a person must pass over a bridge that spans hell and reaches all the way to paradise. If the person has been more good than evil, the bridge widens so that he gets to paradise safely. If the person has been evil, the bridge becomes so razor thin that his soul plunges to his punishment below in hell. If he reaches paradise, he is greeted by beautiful maidens to a place of beauty, light, pleasant scents and an eternity to be lived according to Zoroastrian ethics.

Hell is vividly described in a work called *The Vision of Arda Viraf*, written about 450 AD:

> I saw the greedy jaws of hell: the most frightful pit, descending, in a very narrow, fearful crevice and in darkness so murky I was forced to feel my way, amid such a stench that all whose nose inhaled that air, struggled, staggered and fell....In that place even the lesser noxious creatures are as high as mountains, and these so tear, seize and worry the souls of the wicked as would be unworthy of a dog.[4]

Both paradise and hell will end at a future point in time, according to Zoroastrian thought. All demons will be destroyed forever and the will of Ahura Mazda will rule forever.

---

[3]Yasna 30:2.

[4]Joseph Campbell, *The Masks of God: Occidental Mythology* (New York: The Viking Press, 1964, p. 198)

Scriptures....

Avesta, or knowledge, is the one word used to refer to all the Parsi scriptures. The scriptures used today are frequently known in the western world as the *Zend-Avesta*. The word "Zend" means "commentary." The most important part is called the *Great Avesta*. It contains three divisions:

1. *Yasna* (sacrifice) consisting of prayers offered at sacrificial rites.
2. *Vispered* (all the Lords) containing twenty-four prayers dedicated to the heavenly "powers", used in priestly worship.
3. *Vendidad* (law against demons) including ceremonial law and cosmology.

The smaller part of the *Avesta* functions as the prayer book of the layman, and is frequently called the "little Avesta." It contains:

1. *Yashts*-prayers and hymns in adoration of specific angels;
2. Afringan-rituals;
3. Sizorah-a devotional calendar for each day of a thirty day month;
4. Gahs prayers used in the five divisions of the day; and
5. Nyayish-petitions to the powers of nature.

These holy books thus combine for the practicing Parsi the guidelines for belief, public ritual and private worship.

Parsi ceremonies....

The modern Parsis are sometimes called "fire-worshippers", but this is an accusation they loudly deny. Actually, fire is a symbol to the Parsis of the purity of Ahura Mazda.

Two ceremonies of great importance to the devout Parsi are the Navjote (new priest) and their unique disposal of the dead.

At the age of seven in India and ten in Iran, the young initiate is received into his religion with the investiture of a sacred shirt (sadre) and a sacred thread (kusti). Except when he is bathing he must wear these two items for the rest of his life. The sacred thread or cord symbolizes good thoughts, words and deeds. The kusti is to be tied and untied on at least five occasions during the day as a form of prayer. Four knots tied in the cord symbolize the four elements of fire, earth, air and water.

At the center of every community where there is a significant number of Parsis is the fire-temple. It is kept by one or two priests who see to it that the sacred fire never goes out. Parsi communicants gather there weekly and for special holidays. Parsi children who have gone through the sacred cord ceremony often struggle to see who can have the favored role of carrying off ashes or feeding the fire for the priest. The fire-temple is maintained as a symbol of the purity of Ahura Mazda and his devotees.

Always located near the Parsi fire-temple are the towers of silence (Dakhmas). Burial or cremation is forbidden by Parsi teachings. The dead bodies are exposed to the vultures hovering near the top of the Tower. Burying of the dead is the unpardonable sin.

Upon the death of a Parsi, the body is washed, clothed with a clean suit and wrapped around with the Kusti of the deceased. After ritual ceremonies designed to symbolically clean the body, the body is carried out of the house by official corpse-bearers. These designated persons are the only ones who may touch such a deceased body since it is seen as unclean. An ordinay Parsi not designated as a corpse-bearer would be defiled by touching a dead body.

This principle of exposing the dead to birds has been a part of Zoroastrian life from the days of their founder. As clear evidence of such, the Zend-Anesta demands this procedure:

> And two men, strong and agile, having changed their garments, shall lift the body from the clay or the stones, or out of the plastered house, and they shall lay it at a place where they know that there are always corpse-eating dogs and corpse-eating birds.[5]

This disposal of the dead has caused frequent complaints in such places as Bombay where many Parsi live. In places where Parsis are in the minority and no Dakhma exists, Parsis have on occasion used lead-lined stone caskets to avoid contaminating the soil. These very obvious towers of silence do distinguish the Parsis, however, in communities where a number live.

The future....

The large Parsi community in India is known for its business sense and honesty. This very reputation may prove to be the Parsis religious undoing as interest in material things robs them of their Zoroastrian heritage. The sacred cord, fire-temples and towers of silence remain, however, as the last vestiges of a religion which has had major impact on other monotheists.

BIBLIOGRAPHY

Archie J. Bahm, *The World's Living Religions* (New York: Dell Publishing Co., 1964).

John B. Noss, *Man's Religions* (New York: The MacMillian Co., 1963).

Rustom Masani, *Zoroastrianism: The Religion of the Good Life.* (New York: The MacMillan Co., 1968).

DALOT:

My name is Dalot. I am a fourteen-year-old man who is proud to be called "Zardosti", a word most of the people in my beloved Iran call the followers of Zoroaster, or Zarathrustra. I am glad to be one of the small community of Zardostis in Iran, the land where our prophet-founder lived 2500 years ago.

Some of the more orthodox Moslems here call me Gabar, which means "infidel." Sometimes I do not think this is fair because my family and I believe very strongly in the one true God, Ahura Mazda.

Much of our religious practices are based on cleanliness. For example, when my mother is in her menstrual period, she is not even allowed to hear our holy books read or to touch the children. When

---

[5] *Vendidad Fargard* VIII, c. II, 10.

her period is over, she goes to a public bath house just for Zardosti women where she washes and changes her clothes. Some of the Moslem women say she is risque because she does not wear a veil but she would never defile the sacred elements of the earth.

When I became a man in the sacred cord ceremony, it was a proud day for our family. We talk of it often and I am always careful to untie it and retie it five times a day as I pray.

My father is a merchant who does business mainly with Parsi men because the Moslems will not buy from him. Nevertheless, we are happy when we have daily prayer together. As a Zardosti, I look forward to rejoining my family in paradise one day.

SHAH ARAM:
My name is Shah Aram. I live in Bombay where I am the father of five children. I grew up in Iran, but have come here where I can make a much better living as a carpet salesman. My wife helps with the income as well as she is known as the best weaver of sacred cords in all Bombay. Other Parsis come from miles around to buy her handiwork for the Navjote ceremony. She charges about $40 for each cord.

Sometimes I long for my homeland, but I know it is much better here for us. Although we do not have daily prayer and I do not often remember to tie and untie my sacred cord, we still choose more good than evil as a family. Mithras will bless us one day by uniting us with Parsi friends from Iran. I am glad to be free to choose for the good and to know I will be rewarded.

127

Chapter XVIII
Judaism

In many respects, the thirteen million Jews in today's world are part of a heritage that has given rise to two other major world religions, Islam and Christianity. From Judaism, Christianity obtained the Old Testament or Hebrew scriptures; faith in the one true God; Jesus of Nazareth; the Christian church founded and given growth by such Jews as Peter and Paul; the New Testament (almost totally written by Jews); the concept of social justice and social action, stressed by such men as Amos and Jeremiah; and a rich cultural heritage. From Judaism, Islam gained the valuable concepts of monotheism and the holy book. As the father of both Islam and Christianity, Judaism stands as one of the most important world religions. But, Judaism also stands alone — as a great living storehouse of truth in the worship of Jehovah God.

Who Is a Jew?

Rabbis often remark half quimiscally that Jews have existed for all these millenia just to debate the question of "Who is a Jew?"

In the general public, especially among the Bible-oriented Christians of the United States, "Jew" is usually thought of one of three ways. First, one may hear it said that modern Jews are part of a "nation". However, Jews do not occupy one spot in geography but are spread all over the world. A glaring witness of this is the colony of more than three hundred Chinese Jews currently living in Rio de Jainero, Brazil. Despite the renewed interest in the land of Israel since 1948, Jews cannot be said to be a nation in any geographical sense. There are still more Jews in the Miami area than in Jerusalem.

Second, it might be said that Jews are part of a "race". Sammy Davis, Jr., has been a practicing Reform Jew since 1956. There is a large cology of black Jews in Israel who are from the south side of Chicago. The Eastern European Jew imigrated to the United States to flee the Nazi Holocaust and has certain physical characteristics not at all like the Mediterranean Jew who is in fewer numbers in North America. These are examples enough to make it clear that Jews do not constitute a race.

A third choice is to say that Jews are part of a religion. Today this is not a good definition of being Jewish because many Jews are not mindful of organized or traditional religion, but see Judaism as little more than taking an active role in the neighborhood Jewish community. Surveys in the United States, for example, consistently show adult American Jews will participate in a synagogue or temple service during any given week, except for holy week. In fact, Judaism is the term used to describe religious belief and practices within the larger family of Jewry. This is done to accent the fact that many Jews are not religious in any external fashion, but see their Jewish identity more in terms of being a part of a culture.

This separation of religious Judaism from secular-cultural Jewry is demonstrated well in a late 1977 newspaper headline which read, "Death Intensifies Religious Disputes." The first paragraph reads:

> A nationwide dispute between religious and secular Jews intensified Saturday after a man was killed when his jeep hit a barricade set up by rabbis who regard traffic as a desecration of the holy day of rest.[1]

The best definition of the word "Jew" might be as part of a "people." Anthropologists use this term to denote a social grouping with loosely defined rules of membership. The Jews may be said to be part of a "people" because they share a common heritage of struggle and leadership by God and they believe that their future will be determined together as a group.

As part of a "people", the Jewish share common possessions. They are listed next and constitute the bulk of the remainder of this chapter.

1) *A common history....*

Although Jewish peoplehood dates back at least to the time of Moses for its origin, what is identifiable as "Judaism" comes much later. The history of Jewish identity goes back as far as their forefather, Abraham, who heard God say:

> As for you, leave your land, your relatives and your father's household for a land I will show you, and I will make you a great nation. I will bless you and make your name famous and you shall be a blessing. I will bless those who bless you and upon him who insults you I will put my curse. Also, in you all the families of the earth shall be blessed. (Genesis 12:1-3, Berkeley translation)

A few centuries later God took a confused and despairing group of Hapiru slaves from Egypt and made a covenant with them to be their god. Time after time many of the Jews rebelled and were unfaithful to a loving God. Yet, the people Israel became a powerful and cohesive little nation under David and Solomon. The kingdom, however, began to break down until finally conquerer after conqueror ravaged the land the Jews called "promised."

"Judaism" as such began to crystallize during and after the exile. The Jews returned to Jerusalem from Babylon in a series of migrations beginning in 538 BC. After a century later under Ezra and Nehemiah, the early structure of Judaism was completed. New furnishings would be added later in Jewish history, but the basic foundation was laid by about 400 BC.

The "Judaism" which Ezra and Nehemiah established was quite legalistic. Its chief leaders were priests, and its infallible guide was the book of the Law, or Torah. It was concerned mainly with ritual and

---

[1] *The Times-Picayune*, Sunday, July 2, 1977, Section 1, p.3

ceremonial cleanliness and emphasized careful obedience to scriptural law. It was racially and religiously exclusive.

Judaism's center continued in Israel with developments under Greek and Roman domination and with a period of Maccabean independence sandwiched in between.

From the Christian perspective, when it came time to reveal his young prince of glory, God chose to have Jesus born a Jew. Jesus was proud, yet critical, of his Jewish heritage. In Matthew 1, of the Christian scriptures, Jesus' birth as a Jew is recorded with emphasis on his Jewish heritage. Jesus was circumcised according to God's covenant with Abraham. Jesus prayed as a Jew and often attended synagogues and the Temple for worship. He was later crucified as a Jew and was buried according to Jewish custom. Again, according to Christian beliefs, Christ arose to fulfill the hope the future resurrection of the Jews.

After the Christian era dawned through Jesus of Nazareth, the seething emotions and messianic expectations erupted in Jewish rebellion against the Romans. The result was the slaughter too horrible to describe which accompanied the destruction of Jerusalem by Titus in 70 AD. Unfortunately, many American Christians have thought that Jewish history also died there. This is not at all the case. A dispersion of the Jews followed the fall of the Temple as they spread throughout the ancient world. But the center of Jewish religious and intellectual strength continued in Israel until about 400 AD.

Gradually, however, Jewish intellectual life in Babylon gained prominence and a new center developed. It was here that the *Talmud* was completed about 500 AD. It had been started in Israel.

Meanwhile, a large Jewish community was growing in Spain. Following the capture of most of Spain by the Moslems in the eighth century, a new golden age of Jewish history occurred in Spain. Because the Moslems were fairly tolerant of the Jews, viewing them as "a people of the book", Jewish literature, philosophy and theology began to flourish. For example, Moses Maimonides was born in Spain in 1135. He wrote "Thirteen Cardinal Principles" which became a creed for many Jews.

After Spain came into Christian hands, persecution of the Jews intensified. The Golden Age for Jewry in Spain ended in 1492. The Jews began to flee to Eastern Europe.

In places in Europe where they remained, such as in Germany, the Jews were forced to live in segregated quarters in the inferior sections of town, called "ghettos." Unfortunately, even protestant reformer Martin Luther compounded the hatred and persecution of the Jews by Christians. In 1542, he wrote and published a pamphlet entitled, "Concerning the Jews and Their Lies." Luther demanded that the Jewish houses and synagogues be destroyed and that the Jews be placed in forced labor camps and be kept from practicing their religion.

In ghettos across Europe, Jews were compelled to wear an identifying "Jew Badge", or patch, on their garments, and to remain within their ghettos at night. Understandably, the result was a ghetto mentality, a paranoid defensive attitude by which some Jews came to approve of their isolation from the world about them. This mentality was strengthened by such terrible massacres as the slaughter of a half million Jews by the Cossacks in seventeenth century Poland.

However, through the leadership of great men like Moses Mendellsohn (1729-1786) of Germany, many Jews were freed from the ghetto mentality and took their deserved place in the world of culture.

Even so, the Jews were by no means through with persecution. The worst was yet to come. One of the worst blots in the history of modern man is the murder of six million Jews (abut the same number living in the United States today) by the Nazi's under the madman Adolf Hitler. Most Christians stood idly by while Jews were put to death in the Nazi holocaust.

In the past third of a century, many Jews have fled to America where they have found a home. Others have gone to Israel where they founded a state. The world Jewish community is determined today that they will keep a homeland and have freedom to worship. If this is accomplished, it will be a direct departure from the past. This task is made even more difficult because occasionally anti-Semitism (hatred of and prejudice toward Jews) rears its ugly head.

2) *Jewish beliefs....*

The beliefs of Judaism are based largely on the Shema, "Hear, O Israel, the Lord Our God, the Lord is One." Also, many Jewish homes have a Mezzuzah on the doorpost, which is a small case containing in printed form the words, "Thou shalt love the Lord thy God with all thy heart." The Jews have no creed as such. These two sayings, however, form the basis for much of Jewish thought.

For the Jew, God alone is the answer to why there are human beings and why there is a universe. The Hebrew scriptures give indication of this by starting, "In the beginning God created the heavens and the earth." God is the holy Creator who is perfect in that he is all-powerful, all-loving and all-knowing. The God of the Jews is also vitally interested in the affairs of humans. He even takes the initiative before persons to show his love. In return, God asks for a favorable response from the highest of his creation, human beings.

This same eternal God made a special covenant with his chosen people, the Jews. The Decalogue, or Ten Commandments, functions as the contract for this agreement. These ten statements call for human allegiance to God as the only true God.

Man is to see in God a heavenly Father and companion who is concerned for his fate and does not leave him alone. Man relates to God through this covenant. As a result, the Jews have set up festivals and holy days to celebrate the fact that God is Creator, Sustainer and Redeemer. This is due to the fact that Israel saw itself as elected by God to serve, not to be revered as in some special privilege. As indicated in Isaiah 42:2, the Jewish people follow God's call to serve," I, the Lord, have called you in righteousness; I will hold your hand and guard you and give you as a covenant for the people, as a light to the Gentiles." (Berkeley version).

The Hebrew Scriptures reflect the fact that Jews are acutely aware of the limitations of man. They record that man was made from dust. Yet, they recognize man as God's highest creation. They are forced to ask, "What is man that Thou art mindful of him, or the son of man that Thou carest for him? Yet Thou hast made him a little less than heavenly beings." (Psalm 8:4-5, Berkeley). Thus, the Jewish view of man is as both sinner and the highest of creation.

The Jews are a people of the book, dependent on sacred scriptures for their belief system. Yet, not all parts of the Hebrew Scriptures are considered as of equal value. Among observant Jews, the Torah, or the first five books of Moses, is regarded as so absolutely and fully inspired that every letter and phrase bears the mark of its divine origin. Inspiration to a lesser degree is given to the Prophets. Further, the *Talmud* is given much attention. The *Talmud* is a commentary on the Hebrew Scriptures, particularly the Torah. There are two *Talmuds*, one compiled in Israel and one in Babylon. The Babylonian *Talmud* is used most often. The *Talmud* is divided into two parts; the laws and thoughts on the laws. The *Talmud* reflects the serious view which Jews take toward the laws of God.

The Jews have a strong heritage of social justice and concern. They see beyond responsibility for their individual lives. The strong prophet, Amos, is a prime example of the repeated emphasis on togetherness among God's people. Who can forget his words, "Seek good and not evil, that you may live; so shall the Lord, the God of hosts, be with you, as you say, Hate evil and love good. Place justice up high in the gate." (Amos 5:14-15, Berkeley).

These common beliefs are characteristic of most Jews, but there is nothing one *has* to believe in order to be a Jew. Toleration of divergent ideas is a part of the continuing existence and genius of Judaism. However, these common tenets about God, man, holy scriptures and social justice help to make up the common fabric of Jewish thought.

3) *Common observances....*

Traditionally Jews are a very observant people. They are aware that God is in their life as a people and that he has cared for them through their long history as Jews. On a number of days during the year, these observant Jews gather in their home, temple or synagogue to be reminded of God's role in their lives.

Rosh Hashanah in Hebrew means, "first, or head of the year" and occurs annually in autumn. Heavy emphasis is placed on God's judgment during this ten-day observance. Prayers are made asking forgiveness and for a year of peace and righteous living. A synagogue service is usually held every morning during *Rosh Hashanah*. The liturgy of this New Year's service contains this statement, "On this day, sentence is pronounced upon countries which of them is destined to the sword and which to peace, which to famine and which to plenty; and each separate creature is visited thereon, and recorded for life or for death."[2]

---

[2]Quoted from H.D. Levner's "Judaism", in *The World's Religions*, Norman Adherson (editor) (Grand Rapids, Eerdmans, 1950) p. 75

The last day of *Rosh Hashanah* is called Yom Kippur or "The Day of Atonement." This day is spent in prayer, worship and fasting. Forgiveness is asked for any sins an individual may have committed against anyone in the human family. Four times throughout the day a catalog of twenty-four definite transgressions is recited, followed by a further listing of these sins for which certain sacrifices were offered in the ancient days of the Temple.

Four days following *Yom Kippur* comes *Succoth*, a joyous occasion celebrating the handship of their forefathers who lived in tents or booths (succoth) while in the wilderness for forty years. *Succoth* is also a time of thanksgiving for beautiful harvests. Its last day is an occasion of rejoicing, especially among the young, and marks the point at which the annual reading of the Torah is started anew.

About the time Christians are thinking about Christmas, observant Jews are celebrating Hanukkah. This period celebrates the victory of the Maccabeans over the Syrian-Greeks. Judas Maccabeus led his army into Jerusalem and reclaimed the Temple and purified it for worship in 165 BD. An eight-day festival was proclaimed. The word *Hanukkah* means "dedication". At the center of the *Hanukkah* festival is a candlelighting ceremony using a menorah, or a special seven-pronged candleholder. This ceremony reenacts the legend that a one-day supply of oil kept burning for eight days when the Temple in Jerusalem was recaptured by the Maccabeans.

Purim is the holy occasion which celebrates the story as recorded in the Book of Esther. The story is about Haman, a representative of the Persian king, who ordered everyone to bow down to the king and his gods. Mordecai, a Jew, refused to bow down. Haman became so angry that he persuaded the king to have all Jews executed. Esther, the queen of Persia, was a Jewess. She appealed to the king and Mordecai was saved. Haman was slain instead on the same gallows he had designed for Mordecai. The word *Purim* means "casting lots" and refers to Haman's casting of lots to decide when Mordecai would be killed. Today Jews celebrate *Purim* with merrymaking, carnivals and games. This celebration comes in February or March and is looked toward with glee, especially by children.

Passover is a most important holy period to the Jews. It celebrates the time when God spared his people and destroyed the firstborn of the Egyptians. At the beginning of the Passover, a *Seder* meal is served in the home. The youngest son asks the important question, "Why is this night different from all other nights?" The oldest Jewish male present then retells the story of Moses and the deliverance from Egypt. Special foods are eaten symbolizing the hardships of the Hebrew people in the wilderness. The *Seder* meal is concluded with a prayer of benediction.

At a high moment in the *Seder*, the master of the house breaks a cake of unleavened bread and says:

This is the bread of affliction which our ancestors ate in the land of Egypt. Let all those who are hungry enter and eat thereof, and all who are in distress come and celebrate the

Passover. At present we celebrate it here, but next year we hope to celebrate it in the land of Israel.[3]

Bar Mitzvah in Hebrew means "son of the commandment." When a Jewish boy reaches thirteen, he is called up to the reading of the *Torah* on the sabbath following his birthday. On that occasion he recites the words, "Blessed art Thou, O Lord our God, King of the Universe, who hast chosen us from all peoples, and hast given us thy *Torah*." Family and friends are invited and most stay for a party in honor of the new initiate. *Bar Mitzvah* is a joyous occasion.

As one can see, the Jews are an observant people, mindful of God's leadership in their history and current life. They are mindful also of traditional values and identity as a peculiar people. The Jewish traditions are kept alive only because of the faithfulness of each generation. The keeping of these traditions gives Judaism a continuity not found in some other religious groups and helps them continue as a "people."

4) *Movements within Judaism....*

American Judaism in particular has been shaped by five prominent movements. One of the most powerful is Zionism, the effort to establish and maintain the state of Israel as a home for Jews. Modern Zionism may be traced back to the Dreyfus case of 1894 in Paris, France. Captain Alfred Dreyfus was convicted of treason primarily because he was Jewish. Theodore Herzl, a young writer, attended the Dreyfus and was inspired to publish, in 1896, a pamphlet entitled, "The Jewish State." Herzl called for an international conclave to discuss the establishment of the state of Israel. It was held in 1897, in Basel, Switzerland. The First Zionist Congress called for the establishment of a home for the Jewish secured under public law in Palestine. In 1917, Great Britain announced its support of the Zionist movement. During the 1930's, hundreds of thousands of Jews fled to Palestine to escape Hitler, but this was only about ten percent of the total number killed in Germany in the Nazi holocaust. After World War II, the Jews rejoiced when the United Nations voted to partition Palestine into both an Arab and a Jewish state. The brief war of 1967 was important to Jews because it gave Israel a firmer hold on Palestinian territory. Almost over night tens of millions of dollars was raised by American Jews to support this short war, indication of the vast support of Zionism by the Jewish community in the United States.

Reconstructionism is a movement among Jews to help their people live as Jews in a culture where Judaism does not predominate. Its founder was Mordecai M. Kaplan, an American Jew who formulated twelve principles of reconstructionism. Reconstructionism allows the American Jew to deal with the identity crisis of what it means to be Jewish in the midst of a Gentile culture.

There are three main groups, or "denominations", of religious Jews in the United States. The most conservative group are called Orthodox Jews. They accept the written and oral Torah as the

---

[3]Isidore Epstein, *Judaism: a Historical Presentation* (Penguin: Baltimore, 1959), p. 170

revealed truth of God. The keeping of these laws is the most important aspect of religion. Most Orthodox Jews believe in the coming of an individual Messiah who will bring a peaceful reign to the earth. Most Jews in this tradition believe in the resurrection of the body with a system of rewards and punishments according to one's keeping of the law. A central teaching of Orthodox Jewry is *Mitzvath,* the belief that acts in accordance with God's will enable persons to attain spiritual maturity and achieve due rewards. Central to Orthodox Judaism is the *Torah* and strict allegiance to it.

Conservative Judaism, despite its name, is the branch which has been called "the middle way." Early in this century, the Jewish community in the United States was divided between a rigid Orthodoxy and the reform movement. Conservative Judaism sprang up as an attempt to reconcile the two camps. It seeks to preserve Jewish tradition without being overly rigid. The Jewish law is seen as both binding and yet changing. The Conservative branch of Judaism is larger than either the Orthodox or reform group in America, with almost two million members. Conservative Jews are often reconstructionists also, indicative of the fact that modern American Jews can be affected by more than one of the five movements within Judaism under discussion here.

Reform Judaism is the most liberal among Jewish religious groups in America. Reform was begun in America in 1824 when members of a Jewish congregation in Charleston, South Carolina spoke out for the use of English (not Hebrew) in prayers and sermons. Growth has been steady since this time until it may be said that the United States is the world center for reform Judaism. Lee A. Belford has listed four traits of reform Judaism. They are:

1) Stress upon the ethical mission and teachings of Judaism....
2) Belief in the role of the Jewish people to set such an example in faith and action that they may usher in the Messianic age for all people....
3) Belief in a personal and collective immoratality....
4) Belief in Zionism is optional. [4]

These five movements — Zionism, Reconstructionism, Orthodox, Conservative and Reform — have greatly influenced American Judsiam.

Conclusion....

With the upsurge of Zionism, the "people" called Jews have found a rallying point. They have come to see a land of their own which verifies for the existence of a loving God, the same God who called them millenia ago from slavery into a covenant. Judaism has survived wave after wave of persecution. The future looks as bright as the love of the God they worship.

---

[4]Lee A. Belford, *Introduction to Judaism* (New York: Association Press, 1961), pp. 75-76.

BIBLIOGRAPHY

Lee A. Belford, *Introduction to Judaism.* (New York Association Press, 1961).

Isidore Epstein, *Judaism: A Historical Presentation* (Baltimore: Penguin, 1959).

Nathan Glazer, *American Judaism* (Chicago: The University of Chicago Press, 1957).

Robert Gordis, *Judaism for the Modern Age* (New York: Farrar, Strauss and Cudahy, 1955).

Will Herberg, *Protestant, Catholic, Jew* (New York: Doubleday and Company, 1955).

Nathan:

My name is Nathan. I am a transplanted American Jew who came to Israel last year when I was graduated from the University of Illinois. In Israel, I live on a kibbutz about forty miles from Tel-Aviv. The kibbutz is a collective farm where we grow vegetables and keep a herd of dairy cows. I live in a kind of dormitory and spend most of my waking hours in the fields or studying *Torah*. We have several rabbis here but my favorite is the one who keeps the hot house six days a week. It seems he learns of God through nature. When he teaches us on the Sabbath, he speaks of God as if he were a close friend.

Everyone closes down on our kibbutz for the Sabbath, which begins at sundown on Friday and lasts until sundown on Saturday. It is a day of rest and the study of Torah. Even the cows are milked with machines of pre-set switches so no one has to throw a switch on the Sabbath.

I don't ever expect to return to the United States except to visit for I have found my home here. Please say hello to my friends for me. Tell them Israel is an exciting place to work and live and be Jewish.

Marc:

My name is Marc. I am sixty-three years old. My family and I are the only Jews in a small town in East Texas, where I run the wrecking yard. Everyone in town knows us and we get along alright, except when someone lets it slip that he thinks I am going to "Jew" him down on a price for a used auto part.

I grew up in Poland where in 1939 I saw my whole family shot by Nazi troops. They got me, too, but I escaped from a train headed for the gas chambers at Auschwitz. Sometimes at night I wake up crying or screaming. It hurts to be Jewish, but we are a proud people, and with God's help, we will survive.

When I retire, the first thing I'm going to do is to go to Israel and kiss the soil there. It's going to be good.

Every once in a while I see a rabbi in Dallas and it feels good. In the meantime we keep a Kosher house. On most days it's pretty good being Jewish, even here, but, O God, how I'd like to have my family back.

Chapter XIX

Islam

Islam, along with Judaism and Christianity, is sometimes called a "heavenly religion" because of the three religions' common belief in the one God of the heavens. They are all three said to be monotheistic, or believers in the one true God. These three religions all had their origin in the Near East and have, therefore, certain beliefs and practices in common. Yet, all three have distinct characteristics and deserve to be considered alone.

Islam, the latest of the three, has become the dominant religion of the Arab peoples, but has also spread into Africa and into the western world. For example, the Islamic Center in Washington, D.C., was built in 1953 and is representative of the more than thirty thousand permanent Moslem residents in the United States. This recent rapid growth of Islam, especially in the western world, makes it not only worthy of study, but ever more interesting as its vast heritage of search for Allah spreads west.

Brief history....

Islam did not spring out of religious vacuum. The Arab desert peoples of the seventh century AD were heirs to a rich emphasis on relating to their deities. A form of Christianity, Byzantine, was somewhat known to the people of Mecca and surrounding territories.

The Arabian people were also somewhat familiar with Judaism. Even some of the desert tribes were observant Jews.

Zoroastrianism was also known to a portion of the Arabian peoples. The Persians' emphasis on demons, for example, may have influenced Muhammad's ideas about jinn.

By far the most dominant force in the pre-Mahammad religious life of the Arabian peoples, however, was the native aninism with emphasis on personified force and elements of nature. The pre-Islamic people did worship, on occasion, one god above the rest, whom they called Allah (literally, "the god").

The city of Mecca was a beehive of religious activity. This city is located on the west coast of Arabia and lay on vital caravan routes. Many gods fought for attention there among the residents and merchant travelers. In Mecca was a meteoric stone said to have fallen about 300 AD. The general population saw the stone as a symbol of worship of their many gods. An enclosure was built around it about 550 AD and it was called the Kaaba. It was filled with relics, images and paintings, representative of one god or another by the time of Muhammad. This large black stone was an object of constant strife and profit to the people of Mecca. There was a never-ending struggle to see who could control it prior to the time of Muhammad.

Onto that scene came Mohammad, born about 570 AD. He was of the clan of Hashim and of the tribe of Quraysh, the group that controlled the Kaaba stone during this era. Muhammad's father died before he was born and his mother's death when Muhammad was but a boy left him an orphan at age six. He was reared by his relatives amid the polythesim, (belief in many gods) and desert religious practices of the people. As a teenager, Muhammad became a camel driver and went with caravans from Egypt to Syria. At age twenty-five, Muhammad entered the service of a wealthy widow of Mecca named Khadijah. They were soon married, in spite of her being fifteen years his senior. She bore him two sons and four daughters. Only the daughter, Patima, survived her father.

During his caravan travels, Muhammad came into contact with representatives of the religions and cultures of the world. They all had in common:

1) A belief in one God
2) A dualistic belief in the fight between good and evil
3) A scripture they believed to be the word of God
4) An eschatology teaching that the righteous would be rewarded and the evil punished.

Muhammad began to spend his days in meditation and solitude searching for the one true God. After almost fifteen years of solitude, Muhammad reported that the angel Gabriel appeared to him and called him to be the prophet of Allah, the one true God. Muhammad was told by the angel to go and proclaim the message, "There is no god but Allah." Although Muhammad was unable to read or write, he was said to have received by verbatim dictation the sacred book of Islam, called the *Quram.*

As the prophet of Allah, Muhammad began to preach his new message revolving around the oneness of Allah to the citizens of Mecca. He was not well received. In fact, the residents of Mecca laughed at Muhammad and even later poured dirt on him and his followers as they tried to pray to Allah.

In 619 AD, Muhammad lost his beloved Khadija. In 620 AD, he and his few followers were visited by a few men from Yathrib, a town later renamed Medina in honor of Muhammad. It was located 250 miles north of Mecca. The men from Yathrib were largely composed of Jews who believed that Muhammad might be the Messiah. At first Muhammad turned down their plea to come to Yathrib and bring peace among warring clans. However, in 622 AD, when opposition grew worse in Mecca, Muhammad and his followers went to Yathrib. This famous trip is called the flight, or "Hijirah." It is from this date that the present Muslim calendar is numbered so that 1980 AD is 1258 AD, on the Muslim calendar.

Islam grew in Yathrib, now called Medina. This growth was by no means unopposed, as some of the Jewish clans still prayed toward Jerusalem. Muhammad's influence grew slowly, however, and by 629 Islam had grown into a major military and political force.

In 630, Muhammad with a force of ten thousand men, reentered Mecca as a complete victor. He went directly to the Kaaba where he destroyed the idols and images. By 632 the Moslems controlled almost all of the nation of Arabia.

In that same year, Muhammad died, a victim of poor health. At his funeral, Aku-Bakr, who was to be his successor (caliph) said:

O ye people, if anyone worships Muhammad, Muhammad is dead, but if anyone worships Allah, he is alive and dies not.

Muhammad's successors were called caliphs. By 636 AD, Jerusalem was captured and five years later most of Persia (modern Iran) was conquered. The Muslims entered Spain in 711 AD and continued into France until they were defeated by Charles Martel of the Battle of Tours in 732 AD.

The Muslims entered India in the eleventh century and began to win converts. The modern nations of Pakistan and Bangladesh are the results of this early effort. Islam continues even today to spread, especially in Africa, southeast Asia and the United States.

Basic beliefs....

The term "Islam" can be translated "peace," "submission" or "surrender." The implied meaning is one devotion or surrender to Allah.

The faith of Islam may be summarized in six basic beliefs:

1) *The unity of Allah*

Muhammad stressed the fact of the divine in one God, or Allah, a being who overshadows the universe with his majesty and power. There is no other God, period!

In the *Quran* is found this verse:

Lo! Your Lord is Allah who created the heavens and the earth in six days, then mounted He on the Throne. He covered the night with the Day, which is in haste to follow it, and has made the sun and the moon and the stars subservient by His command. His verily is all creation and commandment. Blessed be Allah, the Lord of the Worlds.[1]

Muhammad fought against the polytheism of his fellow Arabs but equally as hard against Christians and Jews. He taught that the Jews had forgotten their one god and had gone back to the worship of golden calves and other idols. The Moslem prophet thought Christians had perverted their view of the one God by calling Jesus of Nazareth God also. (It had often been noted that the Byzantine Christians with whom Muhammad came into contact in his youth had an unsettled, and perverted Christology and were frequently squabbling over its expression.) Oddly enough, Muhammad urged the acceptance of Jesus as a prophet and even accepted the teaching concerning the virgin birth, but denied strongly that Jesus was God.

2) *Belief in angels...*

Although modern Muslims profess to believe in one God, they give much attention to belief in angels. Gabriel is viewed as the supreme angel because he gave the Koran to Muhammad. Asrafel is the angel who will announce the Day of Judgment by blowing his trumpet. Satan is also considered to be one of the angels. Included also among

---

[1]*Quran* 7:54.

the angels are the numerous jinn, from which the modern English word "genie" comes. Angels were created from fire, according to Muslims, thus the smoke which accompanies the appearance of a genie.

3) *Belief in the prophets...*

Muslims believe that Allah has sent 123,000 prophets to mankind, including Jesus. From this vast number, six prophets are selected as the most important. they are:

(a) Adam, the *chosen* of Allah;
(b) Noah, the *preacher* of Allah;
(c) Abraham, the *friend* of Allah;
(d) Moses, the *speaker* of Allah;
(e) Jesus the *word* of Allah; and
(f) Muhammad, the *apostle* of Allah.

The "seal" of all the prophets, who stands as final in both the temporal and qualitative sense. It is he who received the latest of the revelations from Allah.

4) *Belief in the will of Allah....*

The *Quran* makes it clear that each person is to choose and do freely the will of Allah. In so doing, he may merit salvation. Allah honors these right choices by saving the believer. In the final analysis, man is completely responsible for the choices he makes.

Righteous persons who would win the favor of Allah must submit to his will. A frequent statement among Muslims is in shallah, "if Allah wills it." However, this means that persons do operate out of freedom in their open choices. Allah in his wisdom and mercy allows persons to make choices in the areas in which they will be judged. In all things, Allah's will is soverign.

5) *Belief in the Day of Judgment....*

Depending on how each man fares in the day of judgment, he will be sent to heaven or hell. The Muslim lives in dread of this day because he knows that Allah keeps an account of rights and wrongs and judges each person on that basis. Heaven is located in a beautiful garden with flowing water and plenty of shade. The righteous are given wine, forbidden on this earth to Muslims, but wine in heaven will not disturb the senses and does not leave the imbiber with a hangover. Hell is a horrid place filled with scalding winds, black smoke and polluted water.

The *Quran* describes both heaven and hell with great detail:

These are they who were foremost on earth, the foremost
   still.
These are they who shall be brought nigh to God,
In gardens of delight;
Aye-blooming youths go round about to them
With goblets and ewers and a cup of flowing wine;
Their brows ache not from it, nor fails the sense.
And with such fruits as shall please them best....
But, the people of the left hand,
Oh! how wretched shall be the people of the left hand!
Amid pestilential winds and in scalding water.

142

And in the shadow of a black smoke, not cool, and horrid to
  behold.[2]

These beliefs which bind Muslims together all over the world are
based on the *Quran*. It may be the most memorized book in the world.
It is approximately four-fifths the length of the New Testament.
Ideally, the *Quran* is not to be translated from the Arabic. Instead,
anyone who would know the will of Allah should learn Arabic.

The Five "Pillars"....

The serious Muslim practices his religious faith by means of the
five "pillars" of Islam, so-called because they form the support
system of the Islamic faith.

They are:

1) *Recitation of the creed* [*Shadadah*].

Once in his lifetime every Muslim must repeat this creed in such
faith and seriousness that it is truly his. Many Muslims repeat the
creed numerous times each day. It is by the recitation of this creed
that a Muslim is a Muslim.

2) *Daily prayer* [*Salah*].

The faithful Muslim prays five times daily; at dawn, noon,
mid-afternoon, at sunset and before retiring. The Muslims gather at
the mosque for prayers together on Fridays plus the reciting of certain
passages of the *Quran*. When praying, the Muslem is to look toward
Mecca, his holy city.

3) *Giving of alms* [*Zakah*].

Each Muslim is to give one-fortieth of his income and holdings to
aid the poor. In practice, however, rich persons pay a higher
percentage than do the poor. Those who are to receive this offering
include slaves buying their freedom and strangers and wayfarers. In
modern nations dominated by Islam, the almsgiving tradition may be
carried out through a type of social security program.

4) *Fasting during Ramadan*.

The month of Ramadan is the month when the *Quran* was given and
is observed by Muslims. They must not allow even a drop of water to
pass through their mouths from dawn to dusk during this period. At
sundown, the Muslims are free to eat *Iftar*, the meal for breaking the
fast each day. The only Muslims excused from this fast are the sick,
traveling, mothers nursing infants, and small children. When the
thirty-day period of Ramadan is concluded, Muslims celebrate with a
three-day feast.

5) *Pilgrimage to Mecca* [*Hajj*].

Once during his lifetime every physically and financially able adult
Muslim is to take a trip to Mecca. Annually almost 200,000 pilgrims
do so. The pilgrimage takes place during a special month in the
Muslim calendar called the dhul-Hijah. Just outside Mecca the
pilgrims must leave their form of transportation and walk. During this
month the Muslim must also fast as he does during the month of
Ramadan.

During their stay in Mecca, the pilgram must visit the well of Hagar

---

[2]*Quran* 18:50.

and Ishmael. They must also walk seven times around the Kaaba and then kiss it. They must also make a sacrifice of a sheep or a goat on the tenth day of the Hajj. When the pilgrim returns home he may have the title Haji attached to his name to show his peers that he has fulfilled this religious obligation. It is advantageous for a Muslim businessman to have this title before his name.

These five "pillars" or practices help to unite the Muslim world around the globe. The vast majority of all Muslims will observe the five "pillars", regardless of their allegiance to a specific sectarian form of Islam.

Muslim sects....

Four sects within Islam are important for our study here because of their influence in areas outside traditional Arab territory.

First, Sufism (from an Arabic word "Sufi" which means "wool") refers to those Muslims who are interested in a direct, personal and mystic experience with Allah. The Sufis have been very missionary and have taken the Islamic faith to India, many African nations, Indonesia and the United States. In turn, the Muslim Sufis have been influenced by Christian and Hindu mystics.

The Sufis affirm that although man is not God, he can be one with Allah. Because a person can experience God directly, he does not need books on traditions or arguments about God. This mystic trend has revolutionized at least the Sufi branch of Islam.

In the twelfth century, the Sufis began to organize themselves into monastrial orders, usually centered around a Sufi saint. Around these monasteries was started the tradition of the Turkish "whirling dervishes" who seek oneness with Allah by whirling in one spot for hours.

A second sect within Islam is the Shiite one, who constitute one seventh of the total number of Muslims in the world. Today they are found mainly in Iran and Iraq. The Shiites believe that Ali, the son-in-law of Muhammad, is the one to whom Islamic authority must be traced.

Five out of six of all Muslims in today's world are called Sunnis. They are the orthodox within Islam. Within the Sunnis there are four sects, the largest of which are the Hanafis. They follow the rigid teachings of Abu-Hanifah (d. 767 AD) Americans may remember an incident early in 1977 when Hanafis in Washington, D.C., took several hostages and buildings in order to reinforce their orthodox interpretations of Islamic law.

The "Black Muslims" (their name prior to 1975) today claim more than 250,000 followers in the United States. Only Billy Graham has attracted and converted more people since 1950 than Elijah Muhammad. With the conversion of the former Cassius Clay, the Lost Found Nation of Islam received international publicity for their movement.

Elijah Muhammad was the son of a black Christian minister in Georgia when he went to Detroit in 1929. There he met W. D. Farad, who was proclaiming himself as the second coming of Muhammad. At Farad's mysterious disappearance, the young Elijah Muhammad moved to Chicago where he built a financial and religious empire built on sociological and psychological protest against "white" Christianity.

Before his death, Elijah Muhammad claimed that he knew Allah directly. Further, he taught that all black men are representatives of Allah, and Allah is the Supreme Being among a mighty nation of all divine black men.

A major change in the "Black Muslim" came early in 1975 with the death of Elijah Muhammad, the founder-prophet of the movement. With the takeover of the movement by Wallace Muhammad, the founder's son, members can now salute the American flag, engage in politics, and serve as members of the armed forces. Wallace Muhammad has said on numerous occasions, "Our purpose is the restoration of pure Islam." He has opened membership in the sect to persons of all races. He has also abolished the private police force formerly known as the "Fruit of Islam."

Further, the name has been changed. The sect is now known as the World Community of Islam in the West, or the "Bilalians" in honor of Bilal, Muhammad's first black follower.

The newspaper for the movement has had its name changed from *Muhammad Speaks* to *Bilalian News*. The front-page headline for the March 5, 1976, issue stressed the importance of the new ecumenical spirit among the Bilalians. It read, "Amid World Turmoil Christian, Muslim Unity Grows."

The future of Islam....
The future of Islam is difficult to predict, especially in light of the secularism and modernism of the modern world.

BIBLIOGRAPHY

Kenneth Cragg, *The Call of the Minaret* (New York: Oxford University Press, 1956).
A. Guillamme, *Islam* (Baltimore: Penguin Books, 1969).
J. Schacht and C. E. Bosworth (editors) *The Legacy of Islam.* (London: Oxford University press, 1974).
W. Montgomery Watt, *Muhammad, Prophet and Statesman* (New York: Oxford University Press, 1961).
J. Christy Wilson, *Introducing Islam.* (N.Y., Friendship Press, 1965).

Haji:

Hello, my name is Haji. I am sixteen years old and live in Toledo, Ohio. I guess all my friends call me that because I am Arab and Muslim, even though I have never been to Mecca. My *Imam*, or presider over our local mosque, says that one day perhaps I, too, will be an *Imam*.

Every Friday my family and I go to the mosque for prayers and recitation of sections of the *Quran*. We also listen to our *Imam* as he gives instructions from the *Quran*.

My family and I are part of a fairly large Arab Muslim community in Toledo. We have lots of parties, celebrations with other Muslims. Their support is especially important during such times as *Ramadan* when the other kids don't seem to understand why I do not eat during the daylight hours. It is exciting to be a part of a growing Muslim community in North America.

Muhammad Salaam:

My new name is Muhammad Salaam. Until two years ago I was known as Willie Jones. I am what some know wrongly as a Black Muslim. Our whole name was changed in 1975 when the honorable Elijah Muhammad died.

I am twenty-eight years old and lived most of my life in Birmingham as a black American. Through my religious faith I have discovered a new faith and identity. The new leader of our group, Wallace Muhammad, has brought us closer to mainline Islam, but this has not robbed us of the new pride we have in ourselves.

Worship at our mosque revolves around the study of the *Quran* just as true Moslems do around the world. There is usually a sermon on such subjects as refraining from eating pig meat and not drinking liquor. Next year I am looking forward to going to Mecca.

Chapter XX

The Bahai World Faith

Most textbooks on world religions give little attention to the Bahai World Faith. When they do, it is normally treated as an Islamic sect or offshoot with little merit of its own. However, today this growing worldwide faith deserves full recognition as a significant world religion force. The Bahais do have Persian and Islamic roots, but are more than a tributary feeding a Moslem river.

Who are these people who now number more than one million world-wide? What is their history? Their future? Their beliefs? This chapter sets out to answer those questions, and more....

Bahai history....

A Bahai leader defined the meaning of being Bahai as follows:
"To be Bahai simply means to love all the world; to love humanity and try to serve it, to work for universal peace and universal brotherhood."[1]

The more than fifty thousand Bahais in the United States are part of a world community. The national headquarters is in Wilmette, Illinois, where the nine-sided "House of Worship" was constructed at a cost of more than two and a half million dollars in the late 1920's. American schools for study are maintained in Michigan, Colorado, Maine, California and other states.

Certain practices of the Bahais immediately appear strange to most Americans, including the observance of a nineteen month calendar composed of months with nineteen days each. However, the Bahais' concern for peace and unity continues to capture the allegiance of many Americans despite strange sounding practices and distinctly Eastern origin.

American growth of the Bahais is due partly to Vic Damone, a prime spokesman for the Bahai Faith, who recently spent twenty minutes on the Johnny Carson show telling of his pilgrimage among the Bahais. Other prominent American personalities who are adherents of the Bahai Faith include Seals and Croft, who frequently conduct informal seminars on their religion after their popular concerts.

The history of the Bahai World Faith can be traced to October, 1819, when the person later to be called "The Bab" ("door" or "gate") was born in Southern Iran. In 1844, he declared that Allah,

---

[1]J.E. Esselmont, *Bahaullah and the New Era* (Wilmette, Illinois; Bahai Publishing Trust, 1950), p. 90

the one true God, had exalted him to the station of babhood as a forerunner of a great educator-prophet who was to change the customs and religions of mankind. This declaration brought him and some of his closest followers six years of imprisonment and deportations until his martyrdom at the age of thirty-one in Tabriz.

The great educator of whom the Bab spoke was Bahaullah, who was born in Teheran two years before him. Bahullah announced in 1863 that he was the great manifestation of Allah whom the Bab had foretold. For the next twenty-nine years, Bahaullah lived most of his life in seclusion. He wrote urgent letters to such world leaders as Queen Victoria, the Pope and the president of the United States, urging them to profess him as their lord and master.

Until his death in 1897, Bahaullah produced the spiritual writings which have become the holy scriptures for the Bahai World Faith. All of his *Tablets* are considered equally authoritative as the word of Allah for this new era. As the most recent manifestation of Allah, Bahaullah is the honored prophet of the Bahai World Faith.

In his will, Bahaullah indicated that his eldest son, Abdul-Baha, was to be his successor as the interpreter of Bahai teaching and exemplar of the faith. Abdul-Baha did as his father had hoped. He introduced the Bahai Faith to the western world when he came to the United States in 1912 for a nine-month lecture tour. He was well received, especially in the Theosophical centers. In 1920, he was knighted by the British Commonwealth for his humanitarian activities during World War I. Abdul-Baha died in 1921, having served as leader of the faith for twenty-nine years.

Shoghi Effendi, the grandson of Abdul-Baha, was named guardian of the faith in his grandfather's will. He continued the work of establishing local and national assemblies in many nations until his death in 1957. Effendi left no personal successor, but instead instigated the "Hands" of the Bahai Faith, a group of seventy-three persons who lead the Bahais.

The future of the Bahai Faith is probably a bright one, especially in the western world.

World Bahai membership is currently more than one million in almost five thousand local "spiritual assemblies." If growth trends continue, the Bahai Faith may be a major force in achieving world unity in the twenty-first century.

Bahai organization....

The local meeting group for the Bahais is called the spiritual assembly and elects annually an administrative body of nine persons. There is no official clergy within the Bahai Faith. Rather than being ecclesiastical, these local bodies are designed for fellowship and discussion. These local "spiritual assemblies" in a given nation are in turn coordinated through another elected body of nine members, the national spiritual assembly. Abdul-Baha called also for the foundation of an international spiritual assembly. Bahais live with the belief that this new administrative world order is the model for bringing world unity in the future.

Bahaullah also called for a "house of justice" to be established in each community, and on the national and international levels. This worldwide structure is to serve as the court system when universal peace is attained. This system will supposedly be limited "to matters not covered by the teaching of Bahaullah himself."[2]

Bahais generally oppose other methods of attaining ultimate world peace. For example, the attempt of the United Nations to foster peace will fail because it lacks the "most great peace" of Bahaullah which bases social justice upon religious unity.

Bahais gather every nineteen days for a devotional, business meeting and a time of fellowship in their local spiritual assembly, which functions as the base unit for the foundation of the coming unified world order.

The ultimate aim of the Bahai World Faith is the unity of all mankind, based primarily on the disappearance of strife among religions. Abdul-Baha said, "We must not allow our love for any one religion or any one personality to blind our eyes that we become fettered by superstition."[3] The Bahais blame most social ills, including immorality, social dislocation, materialism and discontent on religious disunity.

Bahais teachd that eventually all "sectarian" churches will be abandoned and replaced by a spiritual center in each community. Those spiritual centers are to be the place for teaching of universal education and will involve the spiritual and moral training of mankind. Eventually this education is supposed to lead to a universal auxiliary language and solution of all economic and moral problems.

The Bahais have a belief that world unity can exist on certain ethical principles. They are pragmatic in their religion to the extent that they believe that loyalty to mankind is the real sign of devotion to God, or Allah. This loyalty is to be shown by concrete efforts to improve brotherhood.

Coupled with this loyalty to social justice is a high standard of personal conduct including abstinence from alcohol (in common with Islam) and other drugs except for medical purposes. Each Bahai has the obligation of daily prayer and an annual fasting period of nineteen days. He is also expected to be obedient to all civil governments and to engage in a useful trade, art or profession.

Bahai teaching stresses that all disease and all other forms of humanity are due to disobedience to the divine commands. A form of fatalism appears in the Bahai teaching that the adherent is to accept with "radiant acquiescence" his lot in life, whether it be riches or poverty. Bahaullah's call for world brotherhood comes regardless of economics, social class or race.

As one can see, the Bahais' ethical code is a rigid idealistic one based on strict moral laws and an aim of world unity.

Bahai beliefs....

For the Bahais, fifteen ideals are upheld as basic:

1) The oneness of mankind.
2) Independent investigation of truth.

---

[2] Horace Holley, *Religion for Mankind.*

[3] Esslemont, *op. cit.*, p. 7

149

3) The foundations of all religions is one.
4) Religion must be the cause of unity.
5) Religion must be in accord with science and reason.
6) Equality between men and women.
7) Prejudice of all kinds must be forgotten.
8) Universal peace.
9) Universal education.
10) Spiritual solution of the economic problem.
11) A universal language.
12) An international tribunal.
13) Extremes of wealth and poverty should be abolished.
14) Work performed in the spirit of service should be exalted to the rank of worship.
15) Justice, as the ruling principle in human society, and religion, as a bulwark for the protection of all peoples and nations, should be glorified. [4]

These lofty ideals are combined by the Bahais with a preoccupation with the role of Bahaullah in relation to such other great religious teachers as Moses, Jesus and Muhammad.

According to the Bahais, the biblical prophecies which speak of the "last days" or the coming of the "Lord of hosts" refer not to the coming of Christ, but to Bahaullah.

The Bahai Faith sees itself as the completion of all the ancient religions. It notes that the Jews await the Messiah, the Moslems await the Madhi, the Buddhists await the fifth Buddha, the Parsis await Shah Bahram and the Hindus await the reincarnation of Krishna. Bahais contend that Bahaullah, as the prophet for this age, completed the messianic expectations of all the major world religions.

The Bahai and Moslem concept of history constitutes the basis for their view of progressive revelation. They hold that history goes through recurring eras and that each prophet, (or "manifestation" in the Bahai case) speaks truth for that given epoch. These manifestations are not viewed as God but do have certain powers and qualities that ordinary human beings do not possess. They are to perform three basic functions: to restate the eternal spiritual truths, to present laws for that particular era, and to release a spiritual force in the world. The Bahais look upon each prophet as an added chapter in the divine book called history. All the major world religions, of which there are nine, are seen as part of one evolving world religion.

Bahaullah declared that he was the educator of all peoples and the channel of a wondrous grace that would transcend all previous out-pourings. He urged all religious peoples to follow him as the latest teacher of God's will. His claims were based on a view of history which assumes that the world is increasingly becoming better educated, both morally and spiritually. Therefore, for Bahais, Bahaullah's teachings supplant rather than supplement those of Christ, Muhamad, Buddha and all other previous manifestations of God.

---

[4]These principles are taken from information supplied by the Public Information Department, National Bahai Headquarters, 112 Linden Ave., Wilmette, Illinois, and from excerpt from a letter from Shoghi Effendi dated March 11, 1936.

One Bahai scholar sums up this view of history:

> The human race is evolving. There was a childhood of primitive man; there was youth; and now we enter the great age of maturity. [5]

This great age, for the Bahais, has come through the teachings and example of Bahaullah.

Especially in those nations where the Christian faith prevails, Bahais are very careful not to alienate the professing Christian. They profess Christ as a great prophet-educator for his era. One Bahai writer says:

> Bahaullah...fully confirms the teachings of Christ and no person is permitted to become a Bahai without first acknowledging Christ Jesus as the Word made flesh...and as the Son of God. Thousands of Jews and Muhammedans (sic) have accepted Christ through the Bahai teachings. Bahais believe that Bahaullah is that spirit of truth foretold by Jesus... [6]

High ideals combined with careful attention to other religions and a prophet constitute Bahai beliefs.

Conclusion....

From its headquarters overlooking a beautiful bay in Haifa, Israel, to its local spiritual assemblies in almost three hundred modern nations, the Bahai World Faith is a religious force to be reckoned with in a world searching for unity.

BIBLIOGRAPHY

J. E. Esslemont, *Bahaullah and the New Era* (Wilmette, Illinois; Bahai Publishing Trust, 1950).

Gloria Faizi, *The Bahai Faith: An Introduction* (Wilmette, Illinois; Bahai Publishing Trust, 1971)

Jessyca Russell Gaver, *Bahai Faith* (New York: Award Books, 1967).

George Townshend, *Christ and Bahaullah* (Wilmette, Illinois; Bahai Publishing Trust, 1957).

[5] Horace Holley, *Religion for Mankind* (Wilmette, Illinois. Bahai Publishing Trust, 1956) p. 82.

[6] Elizabeth H. Cheney, *Prophecy Fulfilled*, (Wilimette, Illinois, Bahai Publishing Trust, 1944), p. 16.

YOLANDA:

I was born in a small town in southern Iran in 1953. My father was a Bahai businessman, who spent part of each year in New Delhi and part in Iran. In our town, we were the only Bahai family in an area dominated by the division between Parsis and Moslems.

We are less persecuted now than before, but I can still remember Moslem boys throwing rocks at my sister and me as we went to school. We were called "Babi", a term of derision.

I came to America where I was graduated from a state college in the midwest with the B.A. and M.A. degrees. Recently I have married an American who has joined with me in the Bahai Faith. I expect to remain in the United States. I consider as one of the main goals of my life the recruiting of more persons who will become Bahai so as to bring about world unity quicker.

ELLEN:

I have lived all my life in Atlanta, where I was born in 1950. Early memories taunt me as they bring back the days when white boys would make fun of my black skin. My parents are still Methodists and attend an all black segregated church.

When I entered college in an all black school for females, my roommate was from Kenya where she was converted to the Bahai Faith from Animism. Her hopes for world peace attracted me to her belief.

One thing I noticed when I attended my first large Bahai meeting was that the crowd was composed of people from all over the world, with all types of backgrounds.

I think I shall always be a Bahai because it helps me feel useful, accepted and part of a vast human enterprise to bring about world peace.

Chapter XXI

Christianity

The man Jesus was a Jew who lived in Galilee, the northern part of Israel. There is far more known about Jesus than such other major world religions founders as Buddha, Zorraster or Confucius.

The four gospels date from the first century and speak of an undoubtedly historical figure. Even the Roman writers Tacitus and Pliny the Younger (about 110-115 AD) speak of Jesus as an historical person.

Jesus was born about 5 BC. His earthly parents were Joseph and Mary. It was through Joseph that Jesus had direct descent to King David. Little is known of Jesus' childhood. He learned to read Hebrew and understood Greek, but his native language was that of Galilee-Aramaic.

Apparently Jesus' father died when Jesus was a teenager. Jesus was left to be the father of four other boys and at least two sisters. This he did until he was about thirty years of age.

It is apparent that Jesus was a popular preacher. His audiences were composed of rich and poor, powerful and powerless and learned and ignorant. His reputation soon spread as a friend of sinners. Even women and children were considered capable of learning by Jesus. His teaching was augmented by healing and miracles.

After two and a half years of teaching in the north, Jesus came to Jerusalem for his final days. He went through several illegal trials and was sentenced to die. He was executed by Roman crucifixion outside the city walls of Jerusalem.

The story does not end there. One Joseph of Arimathea, a member of the Jewish Council, buried the body of Jesus in his new rock tomb. The disciples gave up hope. They refused to believe it when told Jesus was alive. They were convinced when he appeared to them in private and to five hundred at once.

Faith in the resurrected Lord turned the disciples from depression to triumph.

The few open disciples who remained after the crucifixion were joined by three thousand converts on the day of Pentecost. The message soon spread over the known world through the efforts of such persons as Paul and Peter.

By the fourth century the Christians were the most powerful group in the Roman empire. In 311, the emperor Constantine gave toleration to the Christians. Soon Constantine made Christianity the official state religion.

Constantine called the Council of Nicea in 325 AD to standardize Christian theology. The resultant Nicene creed reads, in part:

I believe in one God: the Father Almighty, maker of heaven and earth....And in one Lord Jesus Christ, the only begotten Son Of God: begotten of the Father...One substance with the Father,...Who for...men and for salvation came down from heaven,...was made man,... suffered and was buried, and the third day he rose again according to the Scriptures, and ascended into heaven,... and he shall come again with glory, to judge both the quick and the dead...And I believe in the Holy Ghost....[1]

As the centuries unfolded, the tension between Eastern and Western Christianity grew. In 1054, the Pope of Rome excommunicated the Patriarch of Constantinople. The division was complete and lasting.

Martin Luther (1483-1546) was a German monk who led a moderate reform against the Church of Rome. Luther was one among many who called for moral reform within the church. Because of his opposition to the sale of indulgences by the church, Luther tacked ninety-five theses on the door of the Wittenburg Church on October 31, 1517. They created immediate turmoil across Germany. In them he dared to proclaim that every Christian is a priest.

Near the end of his life, Martin Luther became more conservative. He died peacefully in 1546.

John Calvin of Geneva (1509-1564) was perhaps the most influential mind of the Reformation. He wrote the massive book that became the classic work of the Reformation, *The Institutes of the Christian Religion*. He was virtually the ruler of Geneva, inculcating the people with such values as hard work and simple living.

The Catholic church did not simply sit still and watch its authority erode with the coming of the Protestants. The Council of Trent was called in 1545 in which it was stated that only the Latin *Vulgate* was to be the sure and sacred holy book of the church. The Council also ruled that only the Catholic church has the right to interpret scripture. The Tridentine ruling also confirmed all seven sacraments of the church.

The most important Catholic council of recent times was Vatican II. Meeting between 1962-65, the council made sweeping changes in theology and practice. Non-Catholics were recognized as Christians and the Index of Prohibited Books was abolished.

Sketching Christian history must always be just that — a sketch. The section above has been a summary portrait of the movement known as Christianity just as has been done with the other world religions in this book.

The Christian Scriptures....

The Christian *Bible*, viewed as inspired holy scripture, begins with the Hebrew holy books. Christians regard the Hebrew Scriptures as recording the covenant of God with the ancient Israelites. This collection of thirty-nine books provides Christians with their basic

[1]Selection 740, *The Methodist Hymnal* (Nashville: Parthenon Press, 1966).

premises including: the unity of God, the commandments of God, the responsibility of his people to him and his world, regard for social justice and a bright hope for the remnant who remain faithful.

The New Testament, as currently arranged, begins with the four gospels. However, they came after the letters of Paul to the young churches. Among the gospels, Mark's was probably first. It has been called the "gospel of realism" because it openly presents the humanity of Jesus as he went about teaching and doing miracles.

Luke-Acts forms one unit from the same author. It presents a continuing story of the life of Jesus and the first two generations of disciples after him.

The letters of Paul are named for the people to whom he wrote. Among his several dominant themes are freedom in Christ from the law.

The last book in the *Bible* is the Revelation, or Apocalypse. The book is in the Apocyphral tradition, similar to *Daniel* in the Hebrew Scriptures. It is a symbolic way of saying to first through twentieth century Christians that Christ's way will triumph in spite of present persecution.

Common beliefs....

Modern Christianity is highly fragmented. There are more than one thousand indentifiable sects and denominations dividing Christendom as it enters the 1980's. There are more than 300 identifiable Christian denominations in the United States.[2] In spite of all these division, there are common strands of belief through all of them. They include:

1) *God*

God is seen by Christians to be the cause and ultimate source of this world who is both holy and present in it. He is just, loving, all-powerful and all-knowing. God is seen as Person (not *a* person) who loves, cares, redeems and creates. He is no impersonal absolute existing in space unconcerned about humans, the highest of his creation. Instead, the Christian God is a God of Action, even from the very beginning. The Hebrew Scriptures begin, "In the beginning God created...." From that moment God has been a God of initiative, seeking to reveal Himself to all who will heed. However, Christians agree that God's clearest revelation of Himself is....

2) *Jesus of Nazareth....*

It is in Jesus, the Christ, that God shows himself to be Person, with the demonstrable attributes of love, holiness and involvement. Christians agree that to behold Jesus is to see God in a qualitative dimension not available in any other revelation.

3) *Man...*

Humans were created as the highest of God's creatures but given absolute freedom, they constantly abuse it. As the result of this abuse, humans stand in constant need of a reinstatement of status

---

[2]Cf. H. Richard Niebuhr, *Social Sources of Denominationalism* (New York: Hamden, 1954)

before God. Humans, therefore, live in the tension of searching for good while doing evil. Most Christians can identify with twentieth century Christian martyr Diedrich Bonhoeffer, who wrote:

Who am I? This or the other?
Am I one person today and tomorrow another?
Am I both at once? A hypocrite before others,
And before myself a contemptibly woebegone weakling?
Or is something within me still like a beaten army,
Fleeing in disorder from the victory already achieved?
Who am I? They mock me,
Those lonely questions of mine.
Whoever I am, Thou knowest, O God, I am thing![3]

The Christian affirms that man is what he is because that is the way God created him, in his own image. Humans are, therefore, choosing beings, capable of choosing good, but constantly beset by evil. It follows then that every person possesses dignity and is worthy of the highest respect and active love.

4) *The Bible*...

Christians assert that the *Bible* is the Word of God, a record of God's dealings with humans in history. The Bible was produced by God through a community of faith. In another sense, the present community of faith owes its existence to the Bible. The Bible stands a guide to the Christian life. It reveals the principles of judgment in the light of God's justice and love.

5) *The World*...

Christians affirm that this world was created by God who pronounced it "good." The world exists as testimony to Him who made it. It is ruled in turn by the Creator who runs the world according to his plan. Yet, God allows sin and evil to exist in the world. This evil does not have free rein according to his will, however. He allows evil to exist because he allows freedom. Further, there is an overriding natural law that God employs to govern the universe. Man was given dominion over this world to use it for his own good and ideally for the glory of God. God, in his wisdom, will not allow his final plan for the world to be defeated. It is he who will write the final page of history and rule the world. This is God's world, ruled by a God who allows it to exist along with its inhabitants for a season. Yet, God it is who will ultimately determine its fate.

6) *Eternity*...

For Christians, the culmination of salvation is the final blessing and abiding state of the redeemed called heaven. Hell exists for those who reject the will of God in their lives and who choose instead to live in a state of rebellion against him. Therefore, death is more than an open grave. Christians emphasize the promises of Christ regarding eternal life, such as: "I am the resurrection and the life. Whoever lives and believes in me will never die." (John 11:25-26, TEV). Yet, the Christian knows that there is another sense in which eternal life is a quality that begins now with acts of faith in God through Christ.

---

[3]Diedrich Bonhoeffer, *Letters and Papers from Prison* (London: Fontana, 1953), pp. 221-222.

There is a future judgment in which the faith and works of every person will be judged by the eternal God. An individual's status in eternity will be determined by this judgment.

7) *The church...*

All Christians agree that the church is important for such functions as participating in the sacraments, missionizing, worship, fellowship, teaching and ministering through social action and ministry. Opinions differ as to a theoretical definition of the church, but there is major agreement in the Christian community over its functional definition.

8) *Linear time...*

Christians, unlike Hindus and Taoists, see time as proceeding along a line. Time had a beginning and will have an end. The cyclical view of time, allowing for reincarnation, is rejected by most Christians. Christ stands at the centerpoint of human history.[4] Those who live after his first coming do so in the era awaiting his return. This view holds each person responsible for his actions at the moment. There will be no "second chance" to repeat a moment or remake a decision.

9) *The Kingdom...*

The primary theme of Jesus' preaching was the Kingdom of God. He repeatedly stated that it has several surprise elements which makes Christ's reign different from the normal standards of value in the world. Jesus taught that the Kingdom belongs to the powerless and those who never suspect they are part of it. The normal standards by which the world judges success, i.e., money, fame and power are the Kingdom's antagonist. This emphasis gives a unique flavor to Christian ethics in its purest form.

These beliefs are those upon which most Christians would agree. Christianity lives on in spite of divisions. It is partly because of a common conviction that Jesus of Nazareth was God in human flesh, a historical yet unrepeatable and unduplicated event.

Current trends....

Christianity consistently faces an uncertain future in the light of major controversies which threaten communication between Christians. However, it should be noted that part of the historical genius of Christianity has been the ability to live with differences in doctrine and practice.

At least four crises in faith face Christians as they move into the 1980's:

1) *The Catholic Revolution...*

The 1960's saw the holding of a great ecumenical council called by Pope John XXIII. The council passed decrees and laws which have already begun to revolutionize the Roman Catholic Church across the world. The role of the papacy is being challenged with new emphasis on lay Catholics having more freedom. This breakdown in authority has given a new spirit of freedom for those who are willing to assume new responsibility. The role of priests and nuns is being reevaluated.

---

[4]Oscar Cullmann, *Christ and Time* (Revised Ed., Westminster Press, 1964)

Worship forms have been greatly altered in the Catholic Church in light of Vatican II. Jazz masses, folk liturgies and the use of more music and sermons are being used extensively in some parishes. The vernacular, i.e., the commonly spoken language in a given area, has been substituted for Latin in some parts of the worship service.

The Catholic Revolution has some characteristics which have moved the church in the direction of classical Protestantism. For example, there is a renewed emphasis on the value and role of the Bible in determining faith and practice. The "Dogmatic Constitution on Divine Revelation" issued at Vatican II contains this statement:

> Easy access to sacred Scripture should be provided for all the Christian faithful....the study of the sacred page is, as it were, the soul of sacred theology.... [5]

A second sign that the movement going on in Catholicism is similar to the Protestant Reformation is the renewed emphasis on the role and power of the Holy Spirit. Pope John XXIII concluded his opening address to Vatican II with these words, "To be sure, we are lacking in human resources and earthly power. Yet we lodge our trust in the power of God's Spirit, who was promised to the church by the Lord Jesus Christ."[6]

The lasting effects of the Catholic Revolution will be felt through the new sense of importance of the Catholic laymen. Protestants have long emphasized the priesthood of all believers. The "Dogmatic Constitution On the Church" from Vatican II makes a similar emphasis:

> Let sacred pastors recognize and promote the dignity as well as the responsibility of the layman in the Church. Let them willingly make use of this prudent advice. Let them confidently assign duties to him in the service of the Church, allowing him freedom and room for action. Further let them encourage the layman so that he may undertake tasks on his own initiative....Furthermore, let pastors respectfully acknowledge that just freedom which belongs to everyone in this earthly city. [7]

2) *The Ecumenical Movement...*

One of the most discussed movements within twentieth-century Christianity is the ecumenical movement. Louis Cassels, former chief religion writer for United Press International, wrote:

> While indifferent toward the redrawing of institutional lines, many young people are intensely concerned with establishing warm human relationships with members of other denominations. They have found that Christians can love and respect each other, work together toward common goals and attain a strong sense of community without wearing the same label. [8]

Three uses are often made of the term "ecumenics." The first is to

---

[5] Walter M. Abbott, S.J., (editor) *The Documents of Vatican II* (New York: American Press, 1966) p. 125.
[6] *Ibid*, p. 6
[7] *Ibid.*, pp. 64-65.
[8] UPI.

use "ecumenics" as referring to an organized attempt to join churches or denominations together into one organization. The World Council of Churches was founded in 1948 and is an organization which stresses three goals: Cooperation in common practical tasks, mutual assistance in the field of missions and evangelism and dialogue with a view to unity in faith.

A second way the term "ecumenics" is used is as in "secular ecumenics," i.e., the cooperation of religious groups to accomplish community or social projects. This phase of cooperation is becoming even more widely accepted.

A third way "ecumenics" is used refers to dialogue on matters of doctrine or common concern. Groups meet regularly on local scenes for such purposes. This gives local involvement to the ecumenical movement, one in which all ages and levels of understanding can participate.

Whatever the use for the word "ecumenics," it is further evidence that divided Christians are becoming one in the 1980's.

3) *Role of women...*

Debate rages throughout world Christianity over the role of women in society and the church. On one side of the issue are those who argue for liberation of women by allowing freedom in such roles as priests and ministers.[9] Others argue that women must become more submissive in their role as Christians. One example is Marabel Morgan, author of *The Total Woman*, who argues:

> Man and woman, although equal in status, are different in function. God ordained man to be the head of the family...
> There is no way you can alter or improve this arrangement...
> Allowing your husband to be your family president is just good business.[10]

The controversy continues.

4) *Neo-pentecostalism...*

The presence of more than ten million Catholic pentecostals worldwide is ample evidence that the rediscovery of the Holy Spirit is affecting modern Christianity. The new pentecostalism has certain characteristics, including being:

a) Laity centered

b) With varied licurgical forms

c) Characterized by emphasis on human dignity

d) Transdenominational

The future of neo-pentecostalism is a bright one emphasizing the freedom of the Holy Spirit.

5) *The "new" evangelicals...*

When President Jimmy Carter took office early in 1977, many Americans began to see physical evidence of a new politically involved evangelical Christianity. The term "born again" was introduced into many conversations.

---

[9] Rosemary Reuther, *Liberation Theology*. (New York: Paulist Press, 1972)

[10] Marabel Morgan, *The Total Woman*, (New York: Pocket Books, 1967), p. 82

In December of 1975, an international meeting of evangelicals was held in Mexico City with more than ten thousand delegates. The new evangelicals were well represented. A powerful statement calling for evangelical unity and social action was formulated.

Leighton Ford is a symbol of the new evangelical combining conservative Biblical interpretation with a call for involvement in the political arena. This renewed force is one of the most dominant in current Christianity.

Conclusion....

The future of Christianity is difficult to predict. Problems to be faced include:

1) Growth in the number of adherents to Communism
2) Increasing secularism; and
3) The impact of Christian thought on Christian beliefs.

Holding faith in the midst of ferment is nothing new to Christians. The future holds an even greater challenge.

BIBLIOGRAPHY

Harry Emerson Fosdick, *Great Voices of the Reformation* (New York: Modern Library, Inc., 1954).
Kenneth Scott Latourette, *A History of Christianity* (New York: Harper and Row, 1953).
Sidney Mead, *The Lively Experiment* (New York: Harper and Row, 1963).
H. Richard Nichuhr, *Social Sources of Denominationalism* (New York: Hamden, 1954).
Paul Tillich, *The Protestant Era* (Chicago: University of Chicago Press, 1948).

Magnolia:
My name is Magnolia. I am an eighty-five-year-old resident of Mobile Alabama. My skin is black, which has kept my life interesting, to say the least. The best job I could ever get was as a cleaning woman to some of the rich white families of Mobile. I have outlived my husband now by about twenty-five years. Three of my children are college graduates.

The force that has kept me going through white hate and disappointment is my Jesus. He took the slaves out of Egypt and he's cared for my people all these years. Our church is a comfort to me and I still go to the ladies' society when I'm feeling good. We have a new Reverend down there who can really tell the story. I talk to Jesus all the time. When I tell him my troubles, I know he's listening. A lot of times he puts a song in my heart. Thank you, Jesus. Thank you.

Don:

My name is Don. I play football for the University of Oklahoma as defensive end. Last year, after all my life was dominated by football, I went to a meeting of the Fellowship of Christian Athletes. Fran Tarkenton and Elvin Hayes were there among others. The crowd was made up of a lot of guys interested in sports and Jesus. The speakers were good. One night I was "born again." Later I read that I had joined fifty million Americans who have "found it."

The girl I was dating got really upset. She stayed that way until she was "born again" as well. Before I became a Christian, I was sure it would be dull. It has been anything but that. Jesus has rearranged some of my priorities. Now I am a pre-law student. The other day I was reading in *Proverbs* some verses that make a lot of sense in law.

Chapter XXII

Current Americana

Given the current craze for faddism, the American religious scene changes almost as rapidly as the weather. Names come and go quickly in the rush for instant salvation which characterizes the religion of the American youth subculture.

For example, the Jesus Movement of the early 1970's is but a flicker under the hot search-light of other movements fighting for attention as we enter the 1980's.

To demonstrate how this is the case, one has only to check out those movements which have come and gone in the quarter century since 1955.

The mid-1950's were jolted into religious realization by Olan Watts, a former Episcopal priest, who exposed thousands of American youth to Zen. Zen is covered better in another chapter in this book, but basically is an approach based on experiential oneness with reality, not on ritual or logic or commitment to another person. Zen became the philosophical foundation for the "hippie" or "freak" rebellion of the late 1960's and early 1970's. Zen stresses non-material, non-workaholic values which still threaten those given to traditional American values.

In the late 1950's, along came Timothy Leary and his *League of Spiritual Discovery*. He taught that by dropping acid, one could discover God and self without inhibitions. The street scene bought that premise and some blew their minds while others found their being.

In the mid-1950's came the era of the resident guru. Meher Baba and the Baba lovers tuned in to the proposed unity of all religions while they set in audience with their silent master. When he "dropped his body" early in 1970, it served as only a temporary setback to the Baba lovers who continued their loyalty to their guru of Persian parents born in India and transplanted to America.

Maharaj Ji and the Divine Light Mission made their headquarters in Denver and the famed teenaged guru went from Indian teacher to celebrity as his "premies", or followers, studied his teachings. Maharaj Ji, or "the Perfect Master", presided over the monthly publication of *Divine Light* magazine and enjoyed the adoration of hundreds of thousands.

That adoration peaked in a giant Astrodome rally in Houston late in 1973. Alas, soon the teenaged guru no longer a teenager, married his secretary, moved to California and was disowned by his mother and

163

family as too materialistic. Another guru had suffered from overexposure in the glaring lights of the media and his devotees.

The early 1970's saw a vast interest in the occult world of witches, demons and Satanists. That interest continues and is covered briefly later in this chapter.

With Richard Nixon's interest in China, American youth quickly discovered *The Sayings of Chairman Mao,* or "little red book". Interest soon swung to ancient China and the classic *I Ching*, a collection of future predicting by the divining of hexagrams; i.e., six-line drawings such as follows:

```
————————————————————
————————   ————————
————————————————————
————————————————————
————————————————————
————————   ————————
```

The lines are always interpreted from the bottom up with the unbroken lines seen as masculine, positive forces promising good fortune. The broken lines are feminine, negative and speak of bad luck. So, the hexagram above would be an ancient Chinese symbol of mid-summer, with the first indication of fall being feet.

Interest in Chinese religions led the way to the massive popularity of the martial arts in the mid-1970's, with almost every shopping center location complete with a returned G.I. offering a quick introduction to Karate or Kung Fu (covered more completely in another chapter of this book).

As the 1970's came to a close, American youth were being exposed to a cafeteria of food for thought and action from the eastern world. A quarter century of meditation, martial arts and resident gurus had been on American soil. That soil will never be the same again.

The contemporary scene....

As the United States bursts into the 1980's several religious movements with extra-American roots vie for attention. These may be symbolized by a Hindu guru, a Korean Messiah figure and Haré Krishna chanters.

Transcendental Meditation....

More than one million Americans have been exposed to courses in TM, or Transcendental Meditation. Among them are famous athletes such as Joe Namath, Arthur Ashe and Ted Simmons. Famous TM practitioners also include those from the show world, such as Peggy Lee, Stevie Wonder and the "Beach Boys."

The Student's International Meditation Society (SIMS) reportedly received $18 million in the fiscal year ending September 30, 1976. Growth has been characteristic of the TM movement from the beginning. Its official name of incorporation as a non-profit educational organization in California was changed in 1974 to World Plan Executive Council. (WPEC). Other organizational names in prominent use are International Meditation society (IMS), American

Foundation for the Science of Creative Intelligence (AFSCI), the Spiritual Regeneration Movement (SRM) and Transcendental Meditation (TM).

Part of this growth is due to the fact that educational institutions have been the target of TM efforts. For example, on May 24, 1972, a house resolution (No. 677) was passed in Illinois. It reads in part:

"That all educational institutions, especially those under state of Illinois jurisdiction, be strongly encouraged to study the feasability of courses in TM and SCI on their campuses and in their facilities...."

Educators at Maharishi International University in Iowa now are preparing syllabi and teaching aids for the teaching of SCI at all educational levels, including color video casettes. Founded in 1977, the university plans to open 3,600 centers around the world for the training of SCI teachers. The goal is one training center per million population throughout the world. Each center is geared to train 1,000 teachers by means of a 33-lecture video-based course prepared by Maharishi Mahesh Yogi.

Research on the effects of TM is being conducted currently at more than forty American universities and institutes including the prestigous Harvard Medical School.

Claims for the physiological benefits of TM are broad and extravagent. In a pamphlet produced at the Maharashi International University entitled, "Fundamentals of Progress", such statements as these are contained.

1) TM is a new form of rest, clearly distinct from drowsiness or sleep (p. 21).

2) Meditators perform better on recall tests and learn more quickly than non-meditators. (p. 27).

3) Meditators recover from stress more quickly than non-meditors (p. 24).

4) TM has been shown to significantly increase performance at all levels of work (p. 29).

5) Subjects who practiced TM for an average of 20 months showed a significant reduction in the reported use of alcohol and cigarettes (p. 36). (Fairfield, Iowa. A74)

As a result of these claims, at least seventeen research grants involving TM have been funded by the United States government. They include:

1) A grant from the National Institute of Alcohol Abuse and Alcoholism for $73,000 for training in TM for 30 alcoholics in the D.C. area.

2) A grant of $35,000 for a Title III educational research program for use in New Jersey schools for training 150 students in TM.[1]

---

[1] *Time*, October 13, 1975, cover story.

The advocates continue to work toward reaching the goals of their World Plan, which include:
1) To develop the full potential of the individual
2) To improve governmental achievements
3) To realize the highest ideal of education
4) To eliminate...crime and all behavior that brings unhappiness to the family of man.

A major arm of outreach in achieving this world plan is the Maharishi International University in Fairfield, Iowa. Fairfield is a town of less than 9,000 residents in central Iowa. When Parsons College closed its doors there in 1973, representatives of TM paid $2.5 million for the 185-acre campus with its 72 buildings.

Today the core cirriculum consists of 24 courses, including astronomy, physics, music, western and vedic philosophy. There is a young, full-time resident faculty of almost forty, including twenty-four with earned doctorates. The president is 34-year-old Robert K Wallace.

TM and the Maharishi....

Maharishi Mahesh Yogi says he was born on October 18, 1911, (some say he is older) in Uttar Koshi, India, the son of a local income tax official. He attended Allahabad University, where he was graduated with a specialty in physics in 1942. After working in a factory, he took up the study of ancient Indian scriptures and learned Sanskrit. For thirteen years he was the pupil of "Guru Dev", or "Divine Teacher", Swami Brahmananda Saraswati of Jyotirmath, who presided over Kidarnath, a major holy shrine.

When the Guru Dev was ready to "leave his body", he said to his pupil Maharishi, "My time has come to leave this body. There is only one thing I have not done. Because of the cares and responsibilties of my position..., much of my time has been lost which I should have devoted to achieving the giving of peace to ordinary people. I leave this task to you."[2]

Maharishi is his family name. It means "great sage." He began to do exactly as the dying Guru Dev had requested. He started teaching his special meditation technique in Madras, in southern India. There he trained initiates for six months, who in turn, trained others. The Maharishi soon realized that his was a slow process. So he decided to come to England and the United States to spread his message.

In 1959, the Maharishi traveled to the western world, stopping in Honolulu before going to Los Angeles to set up his movement in the United States. Although he saw great possibilities for TM in America, he settled first in England. After organizing the International Meditation Society, the Maharishi began teaching TM from a modest apartment in London. By 1971, TM was firmly entrenched in more than fifty nations.

Psysically, the head guru of Transcendental Meditation is not very impressive. He is a small man with a long, scraggly beard and

---

[2]Jhan Robbins and David Fisher, *Tranquility Without Pills*. (New York: Bantam Books, 1972) p. 11.

uncombed hair. He wears a white silk dhoti which looks like a white bedsheet. One must be impressed, however, with the Maharishi's happy disposition. He giggles at the most serious times and radiates joy with every statement.

It is no accent that the most powerful figure in the TM movement is a guru from India. This speaks directly to the next question.

Is TM part of a religion?....

An article which appeared first in *The University of Maryland Law Forum* states the official position of TM lecturers which they give at the first of a series of eight lectures, "TM is *not* a religion or a philosophy. Its practice requires no change of life style, no special diet, or any kind of exercise. No special attitudes are necessary."[3]

This is a questionable statement, partly because of the initiation ceremony into TM usually given at the eighth session for the new devotee of TM. The ceremony reads, in part:

...Skilled in dispelling the cloud of ignorance of the people, the gentle emancipator, Brahmananda Sarasvati, the supreme teacher, full of brilliance, Him I bring my awareness.

Offering the invocation to the lotus feet of Shri Guru Dev, I bow down....

Guru in the glory of Brahma, Guru in the glory of Vishnu, Guru in the glory of the great Lord Shirva, Guru in the glory of the personified transcendental fulness of Brahman, to Him, to Shri Guru Dev adorned with glory, I bow down.[4]

This translated excerpt of the hymn chanted in Sanskrit by the teacher during the initiation into TM readily identifies the exercise as a traditional Hindu "puja", or worship ceremony.

This classic Hindu "puja" connects TM with the ceremonial practices of the ancient Indian religion. As one observor puts it:

...Worship of a deity in the form of an image by means of puja is a direct expression of popular theistic religion.... The image in puja is treated as one would treat the god himself in person: it is his murti, his 'form' made manifest for his worshippers. This sense of the deity as a person and the image as his representative form is fundamental to the meaning of puja....[5]

It is important to note that the new TM meditator starts his official involvement with TM in a puja. Not until the ceremony is completed does the new meditator receive his mantra, a secret Hindu Sanskrit word used in meditation.

John White, experienced meditator who has explored the vast field

---

3David E. Sykes, "Transcendental Meditation", Vol. III, Winter, 1973, No. 3, p. 38

4Quoted from, "TM Challenges the Church," by David Haddon, *Christianity Today*. March 26, 1976, p. 15-16.

5Thomas J. Hopkins, *The Hindu Religious Tradition*, Dickinson Publishing Co., 1971, pp. 110-112

of consciousness-raising, tells in his best-selling book, *Everything You Want to Know About TM*:

> TM may not be a religion in the strictest sense, but it certainly is a ceremonial cult with a theological belief system built around a single charismatic figure. [6]

As a form of Hinduism, TM continues as a vital force in modern America. It shows vital signs of future growth because it fills a void unmet in persons filled with anxiety and stress.

The Reverend Moon....

Few groups have caused more furor in such a short period of time than the followers of the Reverend Sun Myung Moon. They may appear as representing one of many separate foundations, from the Holy Spirit Association for the Unification of World Christianity (usually known as "The Unification Church") or the D.C. Striders Club (a track team).

The "Moonies" were first seen and heard in the United States in the late 1960's when the Reverend Moon began to gather disciples by the thousands here. Since that time, they have been most visible, with full-page newspaper ads in major cities and young people collecting money for "hungry children" at busy intersections. Radio and television shows have featured mini-debates between "Moonies" and critical clergymen.

Who are the "Moonies"? Why are they following this Korean messiah figure and who is he?

History....

Sun Myung Moon was born in what is now North Korea in January of 1920 of Christian parents. Mr. Moon attended high school in Seoul, where on Easter Sunday in 1936, he had a vision. Jesus came to him in that vision and told Moon to carry out his "unfinished task." The religious climate in Korea was ripe for just such a message. Some Christians had predicted a Korean messiah who would come in their generation.

After studying engineering in Japan from 1937 to 1945, the young Mr. Moon returned to Korea in 1946 to found the "Broad Sea Church" which immediately had a small following among pentecostals mainly in South Korea.

Alas! another messiah figure by the name of Mr. Paik Kim surfaced. In the town of Paju, Mr. Kim established a community called the "Israel monastery." The Reverend Moon spent six months there learning what was to be the basis of his theology, which he expounded in the *Divine Principle* in 1957.

Between 1946 and 1950, Sun Myung Moon spent time in prison in North Korea for his anti-Communist activity. Late in 1950, upon his release, Mr. Moon and three disciples walked to South Korea where he settled in Pusan and started his new church officially in 1954. His first wife left him at that time.

---

[6](New York: Pocket Books, 1976) p. 138.

In 1960, at age 40, Mr. Moon married his second wife, an eighteen-year-old recent high school graduate named Hau-Ka-Han. This event is referred to as "The Marriage of the Lamb" by the "Moonies" and the couple is called the new Adam and the new Eve, the parents of the universe. It is held that their children herald the coming perfection of humanity.

The Korean following of the Reverend Moon was about 300,000 in 1978. A world membership of more than one million is claimed (the actual figure may be lower) in more than fifty nations. There are about twenty thousand in the United states, including about five thousand "hard core" members.

The future of the Unification movement is a bright one, depending largely on the life span of Mr. Moon, who visited more than 120 cities in 1976. As he approaches his sixtieth birthday, it is difficult to conjecture what the future of the movement will be.

Basic teachings....

The *Divine Principle* is considered holy scripture by the "Moonies". A synopsis of the doctrine found therein reads as follows:

God originally intended that Adam and Eve should be perfect and bear perfect children, but Satan entered into the garden and seduced Eve. By this act, Eve became impure and her blood was forever tainted. She passed this taint on to Adam so that the entire human family became forever impure.

Desiring to redeem humanity from this impurity, God sent Jesus as the second Adam to begin the work of redemption. Jesus was able to achieve "spiritual salvation" but Satan kept him from achieving "Physical" redemption for mankind. Jesus planned to marry and father children, but was murdered by Satan on the cross before he was able to do so. So, mankind's blood remains impure. Today is the day of the third Adam, the time for the physical redemption of mankind and the establishing of Korea as the New Israel.

The third Adam sent by God will marry a perfect woman and their children will be the first of a perfect world. As a result, Eden will return to earth and heaven will be evident here on this planet.

A later book (1974) by the reverend Moon mirrors the thoughts expressed almost twenty years earlier in the *Divine Principle*. One important quote is, "The new history of the world will begin with the arrival of the Lord, who will come as the third Adam. It is the hope of Christianity to recognize, receive and accept the Lord of the second Advent. The change has arrived for all of us."[7]

It must be noted here that the Faith and Order Commission of the National Council of Churches issued a special report in mid-1977 in which Unification thought was analyzed as deviant from Christianity on such central matters as salvation, sin, God and Jesus. On the basis of that report, the Unification Church was denied membership in the National Council of Churches, even on an associate basis.

---

[7]Washington, D.C. HSA-VWC, Inc., 1974, p. 114

Finances....

The financial empire built by the Reverend Moon is remarkable. The Unification Church alone (not counting other foundations within the movement) take in more than $15 million annually. The church owns a twenty-two acre estate in Tarrytown, New York, which sold for more than $800,000 in 1972. That same year, a home for Moon and his family was purchased for the price of almost $700,000. Early in 1977, Mr. Moon purchased a Beacon Hill mansion in Boston for $500,000 and thirty-five acres in Westchester, New York, for $750,000.

The Unification Church in 1978 owned several estates, a large conference center, and a number of apartment buildings, including one purchased at $5 million on East 71st Street in New York City.

One source of the Moon fortune is the selling of flowers and candles on street corners. Mr. Moon himself is the head of a sizeable financial conglomerate in Korea that merchandises and sells vases, ginseng tea, drugs, titantium and other items.

Ethics....

Being a "Moonie" is not easy. Smoking, alcohol, drugs and pre-marital sex are forbidden for members. Even marriage between members is a difficult proposition, since new converts are expected to be in the movement for three years and achieve a high level of spiritual perfection before they are allowed to wed. Marriage partners are then matched by the Unification Church and marriages may be arranged between strangers. This is partly because of the promise given to them of potentially bearing perfect children.

The Reverend Sun Myung Moon sits atop a religious, financial and political empire in 1978. American youth will continue to be attracted to this powerful father figure who promises perfect children.

Hare' Krishna....

The International Society of Krishna Consciousness (ISKCON) claims more than thirty thousand devotees in the United States in 1978. These chanters do not regularly appear in robes as they did in the early 1970's but still roam the streets in search of new followers of one Swami A.C. Bhaktivedanta.

Basic beliefs....

The Hare Krishna chanters believe the following:

The Lord Krishna (a Hindu deity) appeared first on earth about five thousand years ago.

2) There is actually only one God who is known in many cultural forms. The *Vedas*, ancient Hindu literature, gives the name "Krishna" to the *original* personality of God. Periodically, Krishna makes himself visible and invisible at various stages of history. God is pure spiritual energy, but he is a person and has a form but is in no way related to human conception of mundane form.

3) The only purpose of one's life is to give his life to God. Being religious means to develop one's love of God and to serve God.

4) Sin is anything that makes one forget God. Sins as specific acts are basically four in number: meat-eating, illicit sex, gambling and any form of intoxication; including coffee, tea and cigarettes. Such activities as card-playing, baseball and football are viewed as nonsense things.

5) Krishna had 16,108 wives, i.e., he married eight queens, and later married 16,100 princesses at the same moment by expanding himself into 16,100 forms, and had ten sons by each one, or 161,000 sons. All of these marriages were pure relationships and not flawed by lust or material yearnings.

6) The most recent reincarnation of Krishna was the Lord Chaitanya who appeared about five hundred years ago. Lord Jesus and Lord Buddha were also avatars, or representatives, of the Lord Krishna. Krishna will return in about another five hundred years. This time riding a white horse and bearing the name Kalki.

7) The Hare Krishna bible is the *Vedas*, held to be five thousand years old. A single man, Vsayadena, is the author of all the vedic writings.

8) In 1936, a middle-aged Indian named Prabhupada A.C. Bhaktivedanta was commissioned at the death of his guru to preach the message of Chaitanya to the western world. It is said that he chants the Hare Krishna mantra twenty-four hours a day, even once while anesthetized during surgery.

Daily ritual....

The Hare Krishna chanters maintain a rigid daily schedule designed to enhance oneness with Krishna and purity through discipline. The devotees usually rise at 3:30 a.m. to bathe and dress, as personal cleanliness is a part of the ritual. Upon coming from the bath, devotees apply wet clay on twelve places of the body, plus the forehead. There is a separate prayer for each application. The forehead pattern is considered to be the footprint of Krishna.

A worship ceremony begins at 4:00 a.m. and lasts forty-five minutes. This is followed by an hour of chanting on the japa beads, then prayers for the spiritual master. A scripture class in Sanskrit follows another hour of chanting.

Breakfast is served about 8:00 a.m. after the "Aratrika", a ceremonial offering of food to Krishna before each meal.

The rest of the morning on most days is spent cleaning, cooking or laundering. Temple girls clean the altar and put up fresh flowers and candles.

About 11:00 a.m. most of the devotees go out onto the streets to preach, chant and distribute literature.

At 2:00 p.m., the group goes back to the temple for lunch, then back out on the streets for more street work. They usually go to different places, even though they believe that when they have chanted and prayed at the same spot for a year it becomes sanctified.

The evening is composed of more devotional services, supper followed by an evening class, either the study of Sanskrit or devotional yoga.

At 9:00 p.m. there is more free time to study or chant. Many begin to head wearily for bed at this stage, usually only a sleeping bag on the floor. Married couples have their own rooms. The celibate male students share a separate room as do the female celibates.

Even eating is viewed as an act of worship. Food is prepared under strict regulations. It can only be cooked by a devotee, and no one else may enter the kitchen while it is being prepared. The cook is not allowed to taste the food, even to see if it is properly seasoned, and does not dwell on how good it smells. He says to himself as he cooks, "I make this for Krishna." If a dog or other lower animal should see the food before it is offered to the Lord Krishna, it must be thrown away and a new batch prepared because the animal's lust has been aroused.

Only fresh food is used. It is washed well as it is being prepared and no leftovers are brought back into the kitchen. Mushrooms, garlic and onions are never used, for they grow in places of decay and darkness.

At mealtime, a tablecloth is spread on the floor of the dining room and paper plates are set. As the food is served, devotees enter the room, bow low to a picture of Krishna on the mantel piece, their heads touching the floor. Everyone enters and sits cross-legged on the floor. After prayer, the meal is eaten with the fingers. Krishna's plate, the sample of food that was placed on the altar, is passed around and everyone takes some.

A special service is held on Sundays at 4:00 p.m. It is a traditional love feast, with a multi-course meal open to the public. Discussion is encouraged and instruction in chanting is given if desired.

This rather rigid schedule may seem to the outsider to be joyless. The contrary is apparent in every Krishna chapter as the chanters exhibit joy on their way to Krishna.

Conclusion....

The 1980's will reflect the mood of that era. The names may change, but the phenomena will remain the same. American youth will still dance off to the strange music of eastern origin. As the scene shifts, the interested participants and observers will find intriguing the question of how and why Americans are drawn to beads and chants.

BIBLIOGRAPHY

Fay Levine, *The Strange World of the Hare Krishnas* (Greenwich Fawcett, 1974)

Sun Myung Moon, *Christianity in Crisis: New Hope* (Washington D.C.: HWA-VWC, Inc., 1974)

John White, *Everything You Want to Know About TM* (New York: Pocket Books, 1976)

Thomas J. Hopkins, *The Hindu Religious Tradition* (New York: Dickinson Publishing Co., 1971)

Jhan Robbins and David Fisher, *Tranquility Without Pills* (New York: Bantam Books, 1972)

John:

My name is John and I am coming up on my thirtieth birthday. I grew up in a Lutheran home in Minnesota during the fifties and sixties. I have vague memories of catechism even though my Christian background never meant much to me.

I was drafted and forced to serve in Viet Nam. In my first tour over there it was O.K., as I had duty around a compound and the closest I got to combat was shells exploding in the distance. The second time out was not so nice. I got on drugs because all the guys were doing it and I was scared. I was injuried and spent some time in an army hospital where my drug problem got worse.

After honorary discharge and returning to the states, I tried living at home but I could see it would not work after only two weeks. Somehow I ended up in California where I got free room and board and sympathy from the Krishna people.

They trained me to run a printing press and soon I was supervising a printing room where we did some labels for incense and some pamphlets.

Six months later I was chanting and counting beads. Krishna now is my constant companion. He is here now with me. Even though I may look funny to my old friends with my shaved head and bare feet, I feel good and wanted, and increasingly more peace. It is good to be a part of a plan to bring world unity.

Snake:

All I can ever remember being called is "Snake." I will soon be 28, or is it 29. The streets of Philadelphis were my home. Mother comes to see me once in a while in my south side apartment.

Religion to me has always been a turn-on. Zen was a far-out trip for me as I searched for satori. I almost found it before I started doing speed. For a while I found myself in a psychedelic world. Then something went wrong. I was picked up on an illegal possession charge and spent some time in county jails and the state pen. In there I met a "premie" of Guru Maharaj Ji. I actually met him once in Philly, but he left me with literature and I had trouble.

One summer I met some Jesus freaks and lived with them for awhile. They were nice, but so sweet that I was not comfortable.

Lately the "Moonies" have been through here. I might follow them, if I cannot get the bread together to take a TM course.

I've been turned on, tuned out, and mediated around. If I can get the energy together, I'll go after whatever else hits the streets and me next....

Chapter XXIII

Toward Discovery and Dialogue

The study of world religions, as fascinating as it is, can leave the student with a sense of bewilderment. It becomes apparent that diverse beliefs are held by countless thousands whose sincerity cannot be questioned. So, the serious student can throw up his hands in despair or conclude that further study is futile because it only adds to the confusion. The student may also fall into the logical absurdity of wondering whether any ultimate truth exists in matters of religion or the double trap of wondering whether any firmly founded conviction in such matters of faith can be obtained by any person.

Fortunately, the student who has had an *introduction* to the world religions has only begun the journey. He knows, upon reflection, that he has only chopped off the tip of the iceberg. He knows enough now that to stop at this stage is to make a mockery of understanding the human experience around him and his universe.

It is good to report that a student does not have to give up in despair at the close of his first exposure to the ways people on his globe seek to find meaning through ritual and roles.

There are some workable and proven guidelines in finding religious meaning in the midst of the pluralistic calls for ultimate allegiance. Amidst abhorrent and repulsive statements depicting ignorance and prejudice, reflected in such terms as "nigger", "wop" and "kike", the enlightened student can demonstrate an openness leading to world peace.

The alternatives to religious dialogue are not very pretty. They include such current place names as Belfast and Bangladesh and Beirut. In those places strife labeled Catholic-Protestant, Hindu-Moslem or Christian-Moslem (although the root causes may be more cultural than religious) serves as a constant reminder that religious folk who do not talk to each other end up hating or fighting.

There is an alternative to such fighting. It is called "cooperation without compromise" and revolves around certain principles of happy survival. These principles include:

1) Insistence on religious freedom....

Complete freedom of religious choice and the right to propogate one's faith is based on the dignity of persons and the innate ability of each human being to choose freely the religious expression of his preference. This freedom must include the right to spread one's faith, as long as he does so in a manner that allows him to take the offensive

175

without being offensive. From a monotheistic perspective, this right is also based on a knowledge of God, who never forces but rather persuades.

2) *Self-criticism....*

In the field of quest for religious truth, one can never conceive of himself as "having arrived" in his search for spiritual knowledge. This is certainly not true in the sense of having all the answers. Self-evaluation and self-criticism are based on the knowledge that we cannot play God. Even if one conceives of himself as being at one with God as he sees him or it, this oneness in itself is such an humbling experience that he dares not rob God of his prerogatives as judge.

3) *A "middle" mind set....*

In the field of comparing religious options, one may take one of three basic approaches, or "mind-sets". First, he may be "close-minded." This sectarian approach may quickly disintegrate into a kind of "Since I have found truth, you can't have any" approach. In the "close-minded" syndrome, the "other" is to be feared and avoided at all costs. It is held by the "close-minded" person that one can learn nothing from another since that one has a monopoly on the truth. This approach can easily lead to stereo-typing instead of insight. Yet, it is still practiced by thousands of Americans and their international neighbors.

Second, one can respond to the plurality of religious options by being completely "open-minded." However, the student who sees himself as being tolerant can become so open-minded that his brains fall out. He can see religion as a cafeteria line in which he selects one value from one religious tradition and one ritual from another. This selection is sometimes done simply on the basis of what suits him at the moment. Too often this is done out of naivete without adequate informational background. Some have concluded that all religions are about the same without having looked seriously at more than one or two of them. In this case, so-called "open-mindedness" is often a sign of laziness.

There is, happily, a third option. It is the middle ground of being "narrow minded" without the biased overtones that that term often evokes. The person who is "narrow minded" enters into every religious learning situation with certain "faith convictions." He has found these truths to be workable for him over a period of time. These are his "non-negotiables" with which he enters into every religious conversation. The "narrow-minded" one is so secure in his faith presuppositions that he can lay these out candidly and with willingness for re-examination but he is not likely to sacrifice them readily without being convinced both intellectually and intuitively. The "narrow-minded" one says these realities have worked and are working for me. These truths may be sacrificed or abandoned, but not without some personal pain and struggle. This allows him to walk between the extremes of being so "closed" or "open" that he becomes a humanoid without discernment or direction.

176

4) *The total personality....*
In his book entitled *Dynamics of Faith*, the great scholar Paul Tillich has a chapter entitled, "What Faith is Not." He says genuine faith is not overemphasizing any one aspect of the personality. Some groups tend to overstress the mind or intellect, some the emotions and some the will.

An implication of that assumption is that genuine religious faith involves development of the entire being. Any religious tradition which speaks primarily to any one aspect of being while ignoring other parts of personality is therefore invalid. Hopefully, each student of the world religions can find and lead others to religious experience which develops the whole being. The alternative is the syndrome of the intellectually astute but emotionally shallow, or vice-versa.

5) *Positive premises....*
In his helpful book (especially for those from a Christian background), Professor Kenneth Cragg urges the student of the religions of the world to be able to hold "positive premises without negative inferences." This principle in practice allows the student to be positive in his own faith without being judgmental or negative about the religious pilgrimage of other persons. This means being slow to condemn another person's beliefs *or* to label him unlearned, ignorant or backward. This stance means the freedom to be bold and fulfilled in one's own faith and slow to condemn another's personhood or religious pilgrimage.

6) *Common human needs....*
Some who study the sciences of human behavior, such as psychology, Sociology and anthropology, have concluded that human beings are far more alike that different.

One of these scholars is Ina Corrine Brown, who in *Understanding Other Cultures* argues that, while religions tend to divide common quests, there are dominant common human needs. These are at least the need for love, acceptance and community.

There is a common and universal human need for relationship. Religion at its best fulfills this desire by answering how a person relates to God, to his past, the future, his own self-image, society at large, his government, moral and ethical problems and decisions. The intensity of these drives for relationship serves as a constant reminder that the human family has much more in common than in diversity. This does not necessarily imply that all religions are the same, but that the common humanity of all of us unites us in being universally religious.

7) *Conditional exclusivism....*
The principle of conditional exclusivism affords the student of the world's religions the freedom of accepting one's selected prophet or religious model. With this acceptance comes the rejection of a closed particularism that would turn a faith system into a form of idolatry. This allows one to worship a Savior without being committed to a system.

8) *Dialogue....*

The student who desires to continue his learning process will find no substitute for dialogue. He may soon discover that he can learn more by conversing an hour with five Moslems than by reading a chapter on Islam in a good book on world religions.

However, if dialogue is to be successful and beneficial to both parties, certain proven guidelines should be employed. They are:

a) Each dialogue participant should begin with a stance of servanthood. This may even involve the asking of corporate forgiveness on the part of Christians for anit-Semitism in the past. Errors of the past need not be aired in every dialogue situation, but a stance of servanthood, which is willing to do so if necessary, is essential to meaningful dialogue.

b) A second ingredient in religious dialogue is the realization that systems never meet, persons do. There is no walking, breathing Hindu who embodies all the tenets of Hinduism found in any textbook presentation of his religion. Transposing all of one's knowledge of another's faith system on that person opposite one in dialogue shows little human understanding. Humans meet as dialogue participants, none of whom represent accurately or completely their religious tradition.

c) "No holds barred" is a wrestling term which communicates very well across religious lines in dialogue. There should be no forbidden territory. This includes the possibility of conversion by either party. True dialogue involves the right and open possibility of laughing and crying together. The whole range of emotions and intellect is involved in genuine dialogue.

d) In comparing religious traditions and benefits, the dialogue participant should compare himself with the image of God he has as well as with the dialogue partner. Too often the tendency is to compare the marred image of God which he may see in another with the high image of God he has. Dialogue occurs most honestly when comparison is kept to "gods" or between "persons" without interchanging the two categories in an attempt to win a debate.

e) The student of world religions is already involved in the exciting venture which is sometimes called "everyday ecumenics." He knows that the real battles of faith are fought in factories, shops, offices and farms. Occasionally clergymen may imply that lay dialogue is inferior to well-trained theologians in a seminary setting. What some call "brother-in-law ecumenics", i.e., what happens when your Jewish sister marries a Presbyterian, may be the most genuine of all dialogues, even if forced. It is continuing and necessary and some illuminating conversations can occur on a picnic as well as at a seminary.

f) Avoiding sharp personal attack or character assassination is a must if open dialogue is to occur. Modern Jehovah's witnesses do not want or deserve to be reminded by their Chuch of Christ friends of the "Miracle Wheat" scandal involving Charles T. Russell (the founder of the Jehovah's witnesses). One can "win" at dialogue to his own satisfaction, but true dialogue is short-circuited when executed at human expense.

g) True dialogue may be tested by the ability or inability to restate another's case to his own satisfaction, still retaining the right to accept or reject tenets within that case. Such phrases as, "Do I hear you saying?" or "Do I understand correctly when I summarize your thoughts as follows?" will be helpful. Dialogue has *not* occurred until this can be done by both parties involved.

h) Dialogue, to be successful, has to be seen as a continuing process. A short confrontation resulting in frozen impressions is of little value except perhaps to reinforce stereotypes. The conversation must be kept perpetually open, even with the use of letters and notes. To fail to keep conversation flowing is to limit the values of continuing learning about self and others.

Conclusion....

Dialogue is essential in the human enterprise of remaining open and growing. To fail in religious dialogue is to be incomplete.

With that in mind, this book closes with the same poem which started one in 1973:

Who has touched the sky?
Who has seen the day as it went stumbling by?
None but the few
The few who know love by its first name
The color of the heart.
Its first name is God
And no one goes alone to Him.

BIBLIOGRAPHY

Ina Corrine Brown, *Understanding Other Cultures* (Englewood Cliffs: Prentice Hall, 1963)

E. Luther Copeland, *Christianity and World Religions*. (Nashville: Convention Press, 1963).

Kenneth Cragg, *Christianity in a World Perspective*

Ruell Howe, *The Miracle of Dialogue*

M. Thomas Starkes, *No Man Goes Alone* (Atlanta: Home Mission Board, 1973)

Paul Tillich, *Dynamics of Faith*

Clyde:

My name is Clyde. I am nineteen years old and come from a small town in Oklahoma. I have just completed my freshman year in college and am going back home for the summer to drive a tractor for dad. I expect to do a lot of thinking my first year in college and I'm not too sure I'll be coming back.

One thing that bothered me a lot is all that new information I got. For example, there are so many religions that look pretty good. I know my faith and its hard to hold on to at college. So, I've decided not to get confused any more. I asked my preacher about it and he said the main thing is to keep a simple faith in a simple faith. I'm going to do that. No more of those new ideas for me. I guess it's alright to learn about such things, but I can't get confused any more. Besides, I still can't see why Hindus don't eat beef. Or was it the Moslems? Or both?

Jenny:

My name is Jenny. I grew up in Chicago. I am now half way through college and plan to be a dietician.

At times, I get confused about my church background. I have to admit I have not been as faithful to mass as I could be while away at college. Catechism meant a lot to me then and still does. The campus priest is a nice guy who is a qualified counselor and has helped me out of a couple of tight places.

I have had two courses in religion at college. They were both O.K. because they taught me that other people don't think like I do. Besides, I learned about my own faith as I looked at others.

For sure, I don't know everything yet, but is sure is fun (sometimes) to learn about my faith and my world. It could be a lifetime proposition. You will have to excuse me now. There comes my new boy friend. We've got some talking to do. He wants me to go with him to a revival meeting at his church. Is he kidding me? Is he?